family food

photography by Gus Filgate

quadrille

This edition first published in 2005 by **Quadrille Publishing Limited**
Alhambra House, 27-31 Charing Cross Road, London WC2H 0LS

Editorial director Jane O'Shea
Creative director Helen Lewis
Managing editor Janet Illsley
Art direction Vanessa Courtier
Editor Norma Macmillan
Design Ros Holder and Amanda Lerwill
Photographer Gus Filgate
Food stylist Silvana Franco assisted by Anna-Lisa Aldridge
Props stylist Jane Campsie
Production Ruth Deary

Text © 2003 Silvana Franco **Photography** © 2003 Gus Filgate
Design and layout © 2005 Quadrille Publishing Limited

Originally published exclusively for J Sainsbury plc.

Cataloguing in Publication Data: a catalogue record for this book is available
from the British Library.

ISBN 1 84400 216 0
Printed in China

Cookery notes
All spoon measures are level: 1 tsp = 5ml spoon; 1 tbsp = 15ml spoon.
Use fresh herbs and freshly ground black pepper unless otherwise suggested.
Free-range eggs are recommended and large eggs should be used except
where a different size is specified. Recipes with raw or lightly cooked eggs
should be avoided by anyone who is pregnant or in a vulnerable health group.

Contents

Introduction

Meal times in my home have never followed a pattern. Sometimes I find I'm alone with a hot sausage sandwich smothered in mustard, eyes glued to the TV screen; other times the house is packed with my yelling nephews using breadsticks as swords and dropping dollops of cheese dip on the floor. From one day to the next, family meal times vary, not just in the time of day but who's eating and how long you've got to prepare the meal.

The best piece of advice I can offer is be prepared, and whatever happens (and it will go belly-up at times) don't worry about it. Because family meal times are about wholesome, hearty and delicious home-cooked dishes that aren't out to impress but to fill hungry bellies. Enjoy cooking the food and take pleasure from your family's enjoyment of what you give them. And don't worry if the pastry cracks or the cheesecake sinks – real, home-cooked food is charming and packed with personality, and you can be sure that it's going to taste fantastic.

Most of the recipes in this book are really easy and pretty quick too. In fact most of them, certainly in the 'everyday suppers' and 'just for two' chapters, go from shopping bag to table in just 30 minutes. All the recipes are easy to follow, packed with shortcuts and make good use of everyday ingredients, including some good-quality convenience foods, such as ready-made pastry, curry paste and pizza dough mix. And for those occasions when you do feel like pushing the boat out a little and have a bit more time on your hands, look at the 'weekends' chapter, which is full of dishes that are stylish enough for entertaining yet still uncomplicated. There are no huge lists of ingredients or time-consuming techniques here, just scrumptious tarts and plenty of slow-cooked meat dishes.

Many of the recipes in this book belie my upbringing in a large Italian family where daily life focused round the hustle and bustle of the kitchen. My siblings and I would jostle for elbow space on the work surface next to the bubbling pot of herb-scented broth. Like most people, I learned to cook from watching my mum and helping with the simpler tasks. Her classic southern Italian cooking is now incredibly popular in this country and it's influence on me is evident throughout this book. Alongside Mediterranean dishes, you'll find my best English family dishes and lots of quick favourites that I turn to again and again.

There is an old saying in Italy: 'food only tastes good and cakes only rise well if you cook with a happy heart'. I hope cooking and eating from this collection of my favourite recipes makes your heart as happy as it makes mine.

Easy family cooking

Preparation is the key to hassle-free family cooking and the first step is to sort the storecupboard, fridge and freezer. Then assess your equipment, and decide if you need more tools to make your life easier. A little time spent in getting prepared will save you a lot of time later.

Taking stock

Begin by assessing what you have in stock and then having a good clearout. From the storecupboard, get rid of anything that is out of date and ditch multiples of things you'll never use up, like old spices and dried herbs. Be ruthless and throw out anything you know you're unlikely to use, however exciting or exotic. That can of guavas may sound wonderful, but is it going to be opened soon or will it linger in the back of the cupboard until it's past its best? If you really can't bear to part with some dried goods that you feel sure will come in handy, give them one week's stay of execution. After that get rid of them.

The same goes for the freezer. We are all guilty of letting the frost build up next to the ice trays. Now is the time for a clearout. If you must, give the best items one week's grace, but then unplug the freezer, defrost it fully and clean it. After this you can think about refilling it. The fridge is not usually in such a sorry state, simply because it's used more frequently. But most of us could still do with clearing out some of those neglected opened jars of sauces, pickles and pastes taking up space on the top shelf.

When you go shopping, think about what you'll need over the next few days. Decide what dishes you're going to cook and plan your shopping list around them. Also start restocking items you want to keep in store. If you have a well-stocked fridge and storecupboard, and a few standby dishes in the freezer, you'll always be able to feed your family without much trouble.

The storecupboard

Keeping a good supply of essential foodstuffs will guarantee that you can rustle up a speedy supper, however basic. While it's true that many products now can be kept for a long time, it's a good idea to try to keep quantities at a realistic minimum in order to avoid wastage – an average-size bag, can, jar or bottle will do for most families. The only exception to this in my own pantry is canned tomatoes, which I buy by the truckload because I use them so often. If possible have a rack in a larder or cool cupboard for storing sturdy vegetables such as onions, potatoes and carrots that don't belong in

the fridge. Take them out of any plastic packaging and arrange in the rack so air can circulate round them. The following is a list of my suggestions for storecupboard standbys. There are sure to be some foods you wouldn't use and a few missing items that your family wouldn't be without.

Bottles and jars Sunflower oil, olive oil, extra virgin olive oil, toasted sesame oil, white wine vinegar, soy sauce, chilli sauce, Thai fish sauce, curry paste, mayonnaise, tomato ketchup, mustard, honey, wine.

Cans Plum tomatoes, tuna in spring water, anchovies in oil, baked beans, chick peas, cannellini beans, red kidney beans, coconut milk.

Dried goods Spaghetti or linguine, plus a few pasta shapes (penne, fusilli, etc.), noodles, long-grain rice, risotto rice, red lentils, stock cubes, selection of dried herbs and spices, plain flour, baking powder, cornflour, sea salt, black peppercorns, caster sugar, muscovado sugar, sultanas, selection of nuts.

In the chill

Although the storecupboard needs the most careful planning, the fridge and freezer will need some reorganising too. Stock the fridge with your daily basics, plus any special ingredients you need for dishes you're planning to cook that week. You'll no doubt build up a collection of opened jars and bottles again, but routinely check them to be sure they are still eatable. Also carefully look through each shelf and drawer on a regular basis – there's nothing quite as unpleasant as coming across a waterlogged chunk of cucumber. Make sure all food is closely covered, particularly strong-smelling items whose odour could permeate other foods.

The freezer is your saviour when it comes to those bank holidays when you find the fridge is empty by Sunday night, or rainy days when you can't face a trip to the shops. Supermarket freezers are packed with really useful ingredients that you can keep for up to three months and almost everything else you can buy is labelled to show whether or not it's suitable for the freezer. My freezer is never without a packet of flat breads, garden peas, broad beans, mince, frozen pastry, vanilla ice cream and plenty of ice.

However, without a bit of strict management the freezer will easily reach bursting point within weeks of clearing it out. I find the best solution to this is to divide the space in half, and to use one half for fantastically useful ingredients, such as frozen vegetables and pastry, and the other half for dishes I have cooked myself. Every once in a while, I make a concerted effort to eat every prepared meal in the freezer before freezing any more.

Equipment

Having cleared out and reorganised your stocks of food, you can then move on to assess your kitchen equipment and utensils. Apart from cutlery and crockery, you don't usually need multiples of things, and there is a fine line between useful gadgets that make cooking more efficient and other, not so handy items. These are the ones we all have tucked away at the back of the cupboard or drawer or hidden under the stairs gathering dust. Of course our individual lifestyles play a large part in whether or not these tools will ever be used, so you have to decide on this yourself.

I have an electric juicer that's so worn out I'm too ashamed to have it on the worktop. So I keep it in a cupboard and lug it out each time I need it. Indeed, a good way of knowing whether or not to keep a piece of equipment is to position it on your work surface. If after a week it hasn't seen any action at all, then it's off to the charity shop with it. Before purchasing any large electrical items, such as a bread-maker or a heavy-duty electric mixer that's marvellous for making cakes, think about it carefully. These appliances are expensive, take up a lot of room and are only worth having if you are going to use them often.

Here's my recommended batterie of basic equipment. The extras, such as juicers and blenders, are up to you. Remember, though, that many items in a basic kit are multi-functional – if you've got a good non-stick frying pan, why give up valuable cupboard space, and hard-earned cash, for an electric sandwich toaster?

Basic kit

A decent set of knives is a must for any cook. Buy good-quality knives that feel comfortable in your grip and make sure you keep them sharp – I recommend you get them professionally sharpened every couple of months. Before too long, even if you're pretty handy with a sharpening steel, your knives won't sharpen and will eventually need properly grinding.

You also need general equipment such as bowls, chopping boards, a colander, a grater and utensils such as spoons, spatulas and the like. Where possible, especially with utensils, keep just one or, at a push, two of each. No one truly needs two balloon whisks or several slotted spoons.

I think a full set of pans only needs to consist of three saucepans of varying sizes with lids – including a really big one for pasta. Plus a large non-stick frying pan and a wok or large sauté pan. Buy the best you can afford, treat with care and your pans will last you for years.

When it comes to tins for baking, always choose non-stick. For cake and tart tins, go for the springform, loose-bottomed variety as they make it much easier to get your cakes and tarts out in one piece. For individual tarts and muffins, look for ovenproof rubber moulds – as they are flexible, the tarts simply pop out. And make sure you buy sturdy roasting tins and baking sheets – inexpensive, thin baking sheets are liable to buckle in the oven.

Electrical items

All electrical kitchen goods are designed to make your life easier. Although, in theory, you can manage without them, for example by using a mouli grinder in place of a hand-held blender, or a pestle and mortar or heavy chopping knife in place of a mini chopper, the time they save you is invaluable. Most small electrical items are reasonably priced too, though they may have a relatively short life.

Weighing scales It's essential to have an accurate set of kitchen scales, be they electronic, spring-operated or balance scales.

Electric mixer A hand-held electric mixer really does save a lot of time as well as tiring wrist-action. This appliance is inexpensive and easy to clean.

Hand-held blender My wand or stick blender is always on the go for smoothing out sauces and soups. It's a lot safer and easier than pouring batches of very hot soup into the goblet of a free-standing electric blender on the worktop.

Small food processor Okay, so you might not use all the fancy blades but it's fantastic for whizzing up pastry and fine chopping work. If you don't think you'd use it enough, save your cash and instead invest in a mini chopper.

Mini chopper My single most invaluable piece of electrical equipment, this gets used several times a week in my kitchen. It's ideal for chopping small quantities and whizzing up pestos and salsas. A mini chopper is pretty inexpensive, but because the blade is small it does become blunt after extensive use.

Electrical juicer This is one of the most used items of equipment in my kitchen. It works by centrifugal force and the high-speed spin separates out the pulp and delivers you delicious, vitamin-packed juice. The most hi-tech versions extract the maximum juice possible from the fruit but they are very expensive. My cheaper version, though stained and a little dented, still works well after five years of vigorous usage.

family
breakfasts

Italian fried eggs

Serves 1

1 plum tomato, thickly sliced

1 thick slice of ciabatta or other
rustic bread

2 tbsp olive oil

1 large egg

1 small garlic clove, peeled and
thinly sliced

½ small red chilli, thinly sliced
(optional)

large handful of snipped chives

½ tsp balsamic vinegar

sea salt and pepper

1 Heat a ridged cast-iron griddle pan. Lightly brush the tomato slices and
the bread with a little olive oil. Cook the tomato slices first, for at least
5 minutes. When they're nearly ready, toast the bread in the same pan until
nicely bar-marked.

2 In the meantime, pour a little olive oil into a small non-stick frying pan
and crack in the egg. After a minute or so add the garlic, and chilli if using.
Cook for a further couple of minutes, spooning the hot oil over the egg until
it is cooked to your liking.

3 Place the griddled bread on a plate and quickly spoon the tomatoes on top.

4 Throw the chives into the egg pan and splash in the balsamic vinegar.
Season generously, then slide the egg on to the tomatoes and drizzle over the
pan juices. Serve straightaway, with a good cup of tea.

A fried egg is a very personal thing. For me,
the key is a good crispy base, but feel free to
cook yours the way you like it.

Chorizo omelette

Serves 1

8 chorizo sausage slices, each
    roughly torn in half
1 garlic clove, peeled and thinly
    sliced
2 eggs
1 tbsp very roughly chopped flat
    leaf parsley
sea salt and pepper
Tabasco, to serve

1 Heat a large non-stick frying pan. Add the chorizo slices and cook for
2 minutes, then toss in the garlic slices.
2 Meanwhile, crack the eggs into a bowl. Using a fork, whisk with 2 tbsp of
water and plenty of seasoning, then stir in the chopped parsley.
3 Pour the egg mixture into the pan and cook over a high heat for a couple
of minutes, tilting the pan to swirl the egg, until golden and set. Flip over
and cook the other side for 1 minute. Slide on to a warm plate and serve
with some Tabasco for shaking over, and hot buttered toast if you like.

Chorizo is fantastic in an omelette – for this
I always use the pre-sliced variety. Keep the
omelette nice and light – don't be tempted to
beat the eggs with milk rather than water.

Parmesan baked eggs and mushrooms

Serves 4

50g (2oz) butter, at room
temperature
2 garlic cloves, peeled and crushed
2 tbsp chopped chives or flat leaf
parsley

4 large field mushrooms
4 small eggs
6–8 tbsp double cream
4 tbsp freshly grated Parmesan
cheese
sea salt and pepper

1 Preheat the oven to 180°C (fan oven 160°C), gas mark 4. Mix together the
butter, garlic and chives. Cut the stalk out of each mushroom and place the
caps, gill-side up, in individual heatproof dishes. Season with salt and pepper
and dot over the herb butter. Bake for 15 minutes until softened.
2 Carefully crack an egg into each mushroom cap. Swirl a tbsp or two of
cream over each egg and season with salt and pepper, then sprinkle with
grated Parmesan. Bake for 6–8 minutes until the egg is just set, then serve.

Because the cream runs and the cheese melts,
I recommend you bake these in individual
dishes. Serve with hot buttered toast.

Kipper and boiled egg hash

Illustrated on previous pages

Serves 4

230g packet boil-in-the-bag kippers
6 eggs
2 large red-skinned potatoes, such as Desirée, about 500g (1lb 2oz) in total, peeled and grated
2 tbsp olive oil
1 garlic clove, peeled and finely chopped
1 tbsp cumin seeds, roughly crushed
1 tsp dried chilli flakes
1 bunch of spring onions, trimmed and sliced
small bunch of coriander, roughly chopped
sea salt and pepper
lemon or lime wedges, to serve

1 Put the bag of kippers and the eggs into a pan of boiling water and cook for 8 minutes.

2 Meanwhile, thoroughly rinse the grated potatoes and squeeze out as much liquid as possible. Heat the olive oil in a large frying pan and add the potatoes. Season with salt and pepper and cook for 10–12 minutes over a low heat, stirring occasionally. Add the garlic, cumin and chilli flakes, and cook for a further 1 minute.

3 Drain the kippers and eggs. Cool the eggs under cold running water, then shell and roughly chop them. Open the kipper bag and carefully pour the juices into the potatoes in the frying pan.

4 Roughly flake the kipper flesh with a fork and add to the pan together with the chopped eggs and spring onions. Mix well and heat through gently for 2–3 minutes.

5 Stir in the chopped coriander and serve, with lemon or lime wedges.

This is a speedy spin on that all-time brilliant breakfast, kedgeree. I'm a real fan of boil-in-the-bag kippers and I always add the buttery juices from inside the bag too.

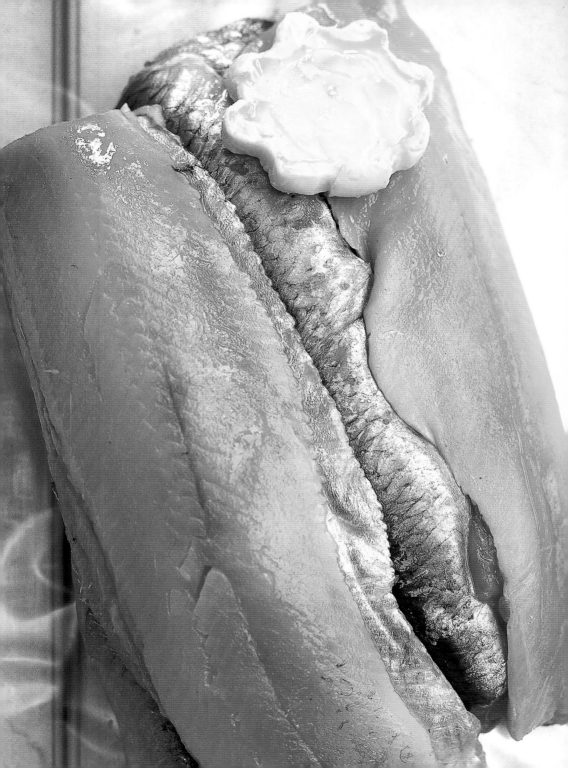

Mozzarella and tomato bagel melt

Illustrated on previous page

Serves 4
4 plain bagels
150g (5oz) mozzarella cheese,
    drained and sliced
2 large, ripe tomatoes, sliced
handful of small basil leaves
olive oil, to drizzle
sea salt and pepper

1 Preheat the oven to 190°C (fan oven 170°C), gas mark 5. Split the bagels in half horizontally. Arrange the mozzarella slices on the bagel bases and lay the tomato slices on top.
2 Scatter a few basil leaves over, drizzle with a little olive oil and season with salt and pepper to taste. Position the bagel tops and press down lightly.
3 Place the filled bagels on a baking sheet and bake for 15–20 minutes until the cheese has melted and the bagels are crisp and golden. Serve at once.

This is a brilliant on-the-way-out-of-the-door bite. Just remember to turn the oven on when you wake up – the bagels can be assembled in moments and baked as you get ready to go.

English breakfast salad

Serves 4

8 rashers of smoked dry-cured
   streaky bacon
½ ciabatta loaf
5 tbsp olive oil
4 eggs
1 tbsp balsamic vinegar
60g (2¼oz) wild rocket
sea salt and pepper

1 Preheat the grill and grill the bacon rashers on both sides until golden and crisp. Drain on kitchen paper and break into pieces.

2 Tear the ciabatta loaf into bite-sized pieces. Heat 2 tbsp olive oil in a large frying pan and fry the ciabatta pieces for 3–4 minutes, turning until crisp and golden all over.

3 Meanwhile, poach the eggs in a shallow pan of gently simmering water for 4–5 minutes.

4 Whisk the remaining 3 tbsp olive oil with the balsamic vinegar and salt and pepper to taste to make a dressing.

5 Drain the ciabatta croûtons on kitchen paper, then arrange the rocket leaves, croûtons and bacon on four plates. Using a slotted spoon, remove the poached eggs from the water as soon as they are cooked and place on the salad. Drizzle the dressing over the salad and serve.

Vanilla eggy bread

Serves 4

4 large eggs
4 tbsp double cream
2 tbsp sunflower oil
8 slices of white bread (day-old)

To serve

vanilla caster sugar, to sprinkle
1–2 peaches, stoned and sliced (or
   other fruit)
150g (5oz) Greek yogurt

1 Lightly whisk the eggs with the cream in a shallow dish. Heat the oil in a large frying pan.

2 Cook the eggy bread two or three slices at a time. Dip the bread into the creamy egg mixture and turn to coat, then fry in the hot oil for 2–3 minutes on each side until golden. Remove and keep warm while you cook the rest.

3 Sprinkle each slice of eggy bread with vanilla sugar. Serve at once, topped with peach slices or other fresh fruit and a generous dollop of yogurt.

I adore this breakfast. Keep a vanilla pod in a jar of caster sugar and you will always have fragrant vanilla sugar to hand.

Sausage, onion and mustard soda farls

Serves 4

8 Toulouse or other pork sausages
1 large onion, peeled and thinly
    sliced
olive oil, to drizzle
4 soda farls
1–2 tsp American mustard
sea salt and pepper

1 Preheat a griddle pan and cook the sausages, turning, until browned and cooked through. Drain on kitchen paper and keep warm.
2 Add the onion slices to the griddle pan and fry, stirring occasionally, for 4 minutes, sprinkling over a little salt and drizzling with a little olive oil as they cook.
3 Split the soda farls open at one end to make pockets. Halve the sausages and put them into the farls with the onion, a little American mustard and salt and pepper to taste. Press the open edges well together.
4 Toast the farls on the griddle for 2–3 minutes on each side. Serve at once.

Make use of the ever-increasing variety of breads on sale to add interest to breakfasts. Here you could use flour tortillas instead of farls if you like.

Pancetta potato cakes

Serves 4

4 medium floury potatoes, such as
   Maris Piper or King Edward,
   about 800g (1¾lb) in total,
   scrubbed
125g (4oz) cubed pancetta
1 shallot, peeled and finely chopped
1 tbsp vegetable oil (if needed)
sea salt and pepper

1 Cook the whole potatoes in a pan of boiling salted water for 15 minutes.
2 Meanwhile, heat a large non-stick frying pan and add the pancetta. Cook
for 3–4 minutes, then add the shallot and cook for a few minutes more until
it has softened and the pancetta is crisp and golden. Using a slotted spoon,
transfer the pancetta and shallot to a large bowl.
3 Drain the potatoes. When they are cool enough to handle, coarsely grate
them into the bowl. Add some salt and pepper and mix well together. Firmly
shape the mixture in the palm of the hands into eight small ovals.
4 Using the same pan, fry the potato cakes for 3–4 minutes on each side
until crisp and golden brown. There should be enough fat left in the pan
from the pancetta, but if not add a splash of oil.
5 Drain the crisp potato cakes on kitchen paper and serve while still hot.

This Italian-influenced hash brown is
irresistible. For a scrumptious weekend
brunch, top it with a poached egg.

Cinnamon pancakes

Illustrated on previous pages

Serves 4–6
125g (4oz) plain flour
2 tsp ground cinnamon
pinch of salt
1 egg
300ml (½ pint) milk
sunflower oil, for frying

To serve
4 large bananas
thin honey or maple syrup, to
drizzle

1 Sift the flour, cinnamon and salt into a large bowl. Make a well in the centre and crack in the egg. Using a balloon whisk, gradually beat in the milk to make a smooth batter. If you have time, leave it to rest in the fridge for 30 minutes.

2 Heat a 20cm (8 inch) pancake pan or non-stick frying pan. Add a few drops of oil and, when hot but not smoking, ladle in some batter. Quickly swirl to cover the bottom of the pan thinly. Cook for a minute or so on each side, then slide on to a plate. Repeat with the remaining batter to make at least 12 pancakes.

3 If you want to cook a few pancakes before starting to serve them, stack them up with a square of greaseproof paper between each one.

4 Serve the pancakes as soon as you can. Peel and slice the bananas. Place the pancakes on warm plates, fold them over and top with the sliced bananas. Drizzle with honey or maple syrup and serve.

Hot pancakes straight from the pan with some
sliced banana and a drizzle of honey make a
fantastic breakfast. These are thin pancakes so
a little batter goes quite a long way: if you
have any pancakes left over, layer them up
with greaseproof paper and freeze.

Raspberry granola

Illustrated on previous pages

Serves 12
200g (7oz) jumbo porridge oats
75g (3oz) desiccated coconut
150g (5oz) pecan nuts, roughly
   chopped
¼ tsp ground cinnamon
1 tbsp sunflower oil

75g (3oz) butter, melted
75g (3oz) light muscovado sugar
3 tbsp maple syrup
To serve
semi-skimmed milk or Greek yogurt
raspberries or other fruit

1 Preheat the oven to 170°C (fan oven 150°C), gas mark 3. Mix all the ingredients together and spread out on a large baking tray, leaving some of the mixture in clumps. Bake for 30–35 minutes until golden and crunchy.
2 Remove the granola from the oven and leave to cool, then break up into clumps. Serve in bowls with milk or yogurt and fresh raspberries.

oven 300 F

Tastier than any shop-bought oaty cereal, this granola can be stored in an airtight container for up to 2 weeks. I love it with raspberries, but it's also good with other fruit such as sliced banana or ready-to-eat dried apricots.

3oz = 85 grams

Potted fruity muesli yogurt

Serves 4

6 tbsp Swiss style muesli

2 fresh pineapple rings, drained and
  roughly chopped

2 x 150g (5oz) cartons apricot yogurt

4 tbsp milk

1 Spoon the muesli into four small bowls or large ramekins. Sprinkle over the chopped pineapple. Mix the yogurt with the milk, then spoon over the fruit. Cover the bowls with cling film and chill in the fridge overnight.
2 The next morning, stir the muesli yogurt well and serve.

You need to remember to put this together the night before, but it takes only a few minutes to prepare. I like to use pineapple but you can use peaches, apricots or berries. The granola (left) makes a good alternative to the muesli.

Banana, apricot and orange blitz

Serves 2
2 bananas
8 ready-to-eat dried apricots,
   roughly chopped
300–400ml (10–14fl oz) freshly
   squeezed orange juice

1 Peel the bananas, break into pieces and put in a blender. Add the apricots and a splash of the orange juice and whiz until smooth.
2 Add the remaining juice and whiz again until thick and frothy. Pour into glasses and drink straightaway.

Get the day off to the right start with a glass of this gorgeous tipple.

Strawberry booster

Serves 1

100g (3½oz) strawberries, hulled and
   halved
1–2 tbsp thin honey
1 tbsp wheatgerm
100ml (3½fl oz) milk

1 Place the strawberries, honey, wheatgerm and a splash of milk in a blender
and whiz until smooth.
2 Add the remaining milk and whiz again until thick and frothy. Pour into a
glass and drink straightaway.

Don't be put off by the name – believe me this
is delicious and it will certainly send you off
to work with a spring in your step.

Mango lassi

Serves 2

1 large ripe mango, peeled, stoned
   and diced
150g (5oz) natural yogurt
150ml (¼ pint) freshly pressed apple
   juice

1 Place the diced mango in a food processor or blender and whiz to a very
smooth purée.
2 Add the yogurt and apple juice and whiz again until smooth and frothy.
Pour into ice-filled glasses and serve.

A classic lassi is simply yogurt, water and
either sugar or salt, to taste. This one is
bolstered with fresh mango and apple juice
and makes a refreshing start to the day.

family
everyday
suppers

Spaghetti with mussels

Serves 4

1kg (2¼lb) fresh mussels
300g (11oz) dried spaghetti
150ml (¼ pint) dry white wine
2 garlic cloves, peeled and finely
    chopped

1 red chilli, deseeded and finely
    chopped
2 tbsp chopped parsley
sea salt and pepper
olive oil, to serve

1 Discard any mussels with broken shells, and those that do not close when sharply tapped. Scrub the mussels thoroughly in cold water and pull out the little beards.

2 Cook the spaghetti in a large pan of boiling salted water according to the packet instructions until al dente (tender, but firm to the bite).

3 Meanwhile, combine the white wine, garlic, chilli and some pepper in a large pan. Bring to the boil and simmer rapidly for 5 minutes. Add the mussels to the pan, cover tightly and cook for 5 minutes, shaking the pan from time to time, until all the shells have opened; discard any that don't.

4 Drain the pasta and return to the pan. Add the parsley and the mussel mixture, and toss well together. Divide among four warm bowls and drizzle a splash of olive oil over each serving.

Every time I make this dish – and that is incredibly often – I'm amazed how quick, easy and tasty it is.

Butter-roasted cod with spring onion mash

Illustrated on previous pages

Serves 6

2kg (4½lb) floury potatoes, such as Maris Piper or King Edward, peeled and cubed

6 skinless cod fillet pieces, each about 150g (5oz)

large knob of butter, plus extra to grease

grated zest and juice of 1 lime

2 bunches of spring onions, trimmed and thinly sliced

4–5 tbsp olive oil

sea salt and pepper

1 Preheat the oven to 220°C (fan oven 200°C), gas mark 7. Cook the potatoes in a large pan of boiling salted water for 15–20 minutes until tender.

2 Meanwhile, cut out six rectangles of greaseproof paper just large enough to sit a piece of fish on. Lightly butter each piece of paper and place on a large baking sheet. Put the fish on the paper and dot with butter. Sprinkle the lime zest over the fish and season with salt and pepper.

3 When the potatoes are almost cooked, pop the fish into the oven and roast for 6–8 minutes, depending on thickness, until just cooked.

4 Drain the potatoes well and return to the pan. Mash roughly with a fork, then stir in the lime juice, spring onions and olive oil. Season to taste.

5 Divide the flavoured mash among warm serving plates. Gently ease each piece of fish off the paper and slide on top of the mash. Serve immediately.

The tricky thing about cooking skinless fish is preventing it flaking apart as you serve it. Cooking it this way, on sheets of greaseproof paper, means you can slide the fish on to the plate without it breaking. The soft spring onion mash makes a perfect partner.

Special fish curry

Illustrated on previous pages

Serves 6

1 tbsp sunflower oil

1 large onion, peeled and finely chopped

2 garlic cloves, peeled and finely chopped

5cm (2 inch) piece fresh root ginger, peeled and finely chopped

2 tbsp hot curry paste

300ml (½ pint) chicken stock

400ml can coconut milk

2 tsp caster sugar

¼ tsp salt

750g (1lb 10oz) skinless white fish fillet, such as coley, pollack, haddock, cod or monkfish, cut into large chunks

400g (14oz) peeled raw tiger prawns, thawed if frozen

juice of 2 limes, or to taste

small handful of coriander leaves, to serve

1 Heat the oil in a large sauté pan and cook the onion, garlic and ginger for 5 minutes until softened. Stir in the curry paste and cook for 2 minutes. Add the chicken stock and coconut milk and bring to a gentle simmer (do not boil as the coconut milk could separate).

2 Stir in the sugar and salt, then add the fish. Simmer for just 2 minutes or so until the fish is opaque, then add the prawns and cook for 1–2 minutes until pink.

3 Add lime juice to taste, then ladle the curry into warm bowls. Scatter over the coriander to serve.

Though very easy, this is a really stylish supper dish – certainly smart enough to serve for a midweek dinner party. Serve with basmati or jasmine rice and mini poppadoms.

Grilled mackerel with lemon mint drizzle

Illustrated on previous pages

Serves 4

4 whole mackerel, each about 300g
   (11oz) filleted
1 small garlic clove, peeled and
   quartered
3 spring onions, trimmed and
   roughly chopped

20g (¾oz) mint
1 small lemon
1 tbsp capers, drained and rinsed
4 tbsp extra virgin olive oil
sea salt and pepper

1 Preheat the grill to high. Season the mackerel fillets, then arrange skin-side up on a foil-lined baking sheet. Cook under the grill for 3 minutes on each side.

2 Meanwhile, whiz the garlic and spring onions in a small food processor until finely chopped. Tear in the mint leaves, grate in the lemon zest, and add the capers and a little salt. Whiz again. Squeeze in the juice from half the lemon and pour in the olive oil, then give one final blitz to blend thoroughly.

3 Place the grilled mackerel on warm serving plates and drizzle over the dressing. Serve immediately.

Mackerel is packed with all the right kinds of oils and it's economical too. These fillets are cooked within a few minutes under a hot grill. Serve them with a leafy salad and boiled new potatoes for a satisfying, healthy family meal.

Haddock and coriander fish cakes

Serves 4

1kg (2¼lb) floury potatoes, such as Maris Piper or King Edward, peeled and diced
400g (14oz) haddock fillet
300ml (½ pint) milk
1 tbsp Thai red curry paste
1 bunch of spring onions, trimmed and thinly sliced

4 tbsp chopped coriander
4 tbsp plain flour, seasoned
1 egg, beaten
75g (3oz) natural or golden dried breadcrumbs
2–3 tbsp sunflower oil
sea salt and pepper
2 limes, cut into wedges, to serve

1 Boil the potatoes in a large pan of salted water for 15 minutes or so until they are tender.

2 Meanwhile, place the fish in a large sauté pan, pour over the milk, cover and bring to the boil. Immediately remove from the heat and leave the fish to cook in the residual heat for 5 minutes, or until it can be flaked.

3 Drain the potatoes well and return to the pan. Mash until smooth, then stir in the curry paste, spring onions and chopped coriander.

4 Drain the fish well. Flake roughly, discarding any skin and bones, then lightly stir into the mash mixture. Season with salt and pepper to taste. Shape the mixture into eight cakes, patting to compact them. If you have time, cover and chill so the cakes firm up.

5 Dust the fish cakes in the seasoned flour, then carefully dip them in the beaten egg, then into the breadcrumbs to coat on all sides. Heat the oil in a heavy-based frying pan and shallow-fry the fish cakes in batches for about 2 minutes on each side until crisp and golden. Drain on kitchen paper and serve, with lime wedges.

This dish offers the best of both worlds – warm fluffy potato and lovely, flaky haddock from our coastline with the red curry kick and fragrant coriander of Thailand.

Spiced chicken with herb cous cous

Serves 4

4 chicken breasts, each about
125g (4oz)
2–3 tsp harissa or other thick
chilli paste
300g (11oz) cous cous
1 red onion, peeled and finely
chopped
350ml (12fl oz) hot chicken stock
grated zest and juice of 1 lemon

2 ripe tomatoes, roughly chopped
200g (7oz) feta cheese, crumbled into
small pieces
20g (¾oz) parsley, roughly chopped
20g (¾oz) coriander, roughly
chopped
3 tbsp olive oil
sea salt and pepper
1 lime, cut into wedges, to serve

1 Preheat the grill to medium. Deeply slash the skin side of the chicken, then rub the harissa into each breast, making sure it goes into the slashes.
2 Arrange the chicken skin-side down on a foil-lined grill pan. Cook under the grill for 6–7 minutes on each side or until the skin is crisp and the chicken is cooked through.
3 Meanwhile, place the cous cous and onion in a large heatproof bowl and pour over the hot stock and the lemon juice. Leave to soak for 10 minutes until all the liquid has been absorbed.
4 Break up the cous cous with a fork, then stir through the tomatoes, feta, lemon zest, herbs and olive oil. Add salt and pepper to taste.
5 Place the chicken and warm cous cous on warm plates and add a lime wedge on the side.

This recipe is based on a dish I ate in Egypt while on holiday. It's very easy to make and the crispy, succulent chicken tastes superb.

Chicken vindaloo

Serves 4

8 skinless chicken thigh fillets,
    about 900g (2lb) in total, cubed
3 tbsp vindaloo curry paste
1–2 tbsp sunflower oil
1 onion, peeled and chopped
10cm (4 inch) piece fresh root
    ginger, peeled and chopped

150ml (¼ pint) dry white wine
300ml (½ pint) hot chicken stock
1 tsp dark soft brown sugar
sea salt and pepper
1 mild green chilli, thinly sliced, to
    serve

1 Place the chicken cubes in a bowl, add the curry paste and turn to coat. Leave to marinate in the fridge for at least 30 minutes, or up to 8 hours.

2 Heat the oil in a large pan and cook the chicken for 3–4 minutes. Add the onion and ginger and cook for a further 5 minutes until golden.

3 Pour in the wine and bubble rapidly for 5 minutes until it evaporates, then stir in the stock and brown sugar. Bring to the boil and simmer gently for 20 minutes. Season with salt and pepper to taste.

4 Divide the curry among warm plates and scatter over the chilli to serve.

Vindaloo is traditionally made with pork and a wet curry paste. This simplified version uses chicken thighs and ready-made curry paste. Serve with basmati rice and simple greens.

Lamb and red onion pilaf

Serves 4

2–3 tbsp sunflower oil
2 tbsp plain flour
1 tsp ground cumin
½ tsp ground coriander
1 tsp hot chilli powder
750g (1lb 10oz) boneless lamb, cubed
2 red onions, peeled and thickly sliced
2 garlic cloves, peeled and thinly sliced
1 red chilli, deseeded and finely chopped
400g (14oz) basmati rice
750ml (1¼ pints) hot vegetable stock
1 tbsp hot curry paste
juice of 1 lemon
sea salt and pepper
20g (¾oz) coriander, to serve

1 Pour 2 tbsp of the oil into a large flameproof casserole and set it over a medium heat. Meanwhile, stir together the flour, cumin, coriander, chilli powder and some salt and pepper.

2 Toss the lamb cubes in the flour mixture, then fry in the hot oil for 5 minutes until nicely browned (you may have to do this in two batches). Remove the lamb with a slotted spoon and set aside.

3 If the casserole is dry, add another 1 tbsp of oil, then cook the onions for 5 minutes. Stir in the garlic and fresh chilli and cook for a further 1 minute.

4 Stir in the rice and return the lamb to the casserole, then pour over the stock. Mix in the curry paste, using a wooden spoon to scrape up all the tasty bits from the bottom of the pan, and bring to the boil. Reduce the heat, cover and simmer gently for 15 minutes until the rice is tender and all the liquid has been absorbed.

5 Stir in the lemon juice and check the seasoning. Divide among warm plates and scatter a few coriander leaves over each serving.

Cumin and coriander complement sweet red onions and lamb in this tasty pilaf. The chilli kick is warm rather than hot, so it is fine for all ages. Serve with a leafy salad.

Spiced lamb koftas with tzatziki

Illustrated on previous pages

Serves 4

500g (1lb 2oz) lean lamb mince
1 small onion, peeled and finely
   chopped
3 tbsp chopped mint
1 tbsp chopped oregano
1 tsp ground coriander
½ small cucumber
150g (5oz) natural yogurt
1 garlic clove, peeled and crushed
1 lemon, cut into 6 wedges
sea salt and pepper

To serve

4 pitta breads
salad leaves, such as baby spinach
   or rocket
small mint leaves

1 Soak 12 wooden skewers in hot water for 10 minutes. Preheat the grill to high. Mix together the lamb, onion, 2 tbsp of the mint, the oregano, coriander and a seasoning of salt and pepper.

2 Divide the mixture into 12 portions and squeeze around the pre-soaked skewers. Grill the lamb kebabs for 8–10 minutes, turning occasionally, until well browned and cooked through.

3 Meanwhile, for the tzatziki, grate the cucumber and squeeze out excess liquid with your hands. Mix with the yogurt, garlic and remaining mint. Add some salt and squeeze in the juice from one or two of the lemon wedges.

4 Warm the pitta breads under the grill, turning once. Serve the lamb kebabs in the warm pittas with the salad and mint leaves, and tzatziki. Accompany with the remaining lemon wedges.

This classic Greek-style kebab is served in traditional style with tzatziki, warm pitta bread and salad.

Barbecued lamb steaks with summer salad

Serves 6

3 tbsp plain flour
1 tbsp dried oregano
1 tsp dried rosemary
1 tsp salt
1 tsp steak pepper or coarsely
    cracked black peppercorns
1 tsp cayenne pepper
6 lamb leg steaks, bone in, each
    about 150g (5oz)
1 tbsp sunflower oil (if using a
    griddle pan)

For the salad

1 cucumber, peeled and cubed
1 small red onion, peeled and
    thinly sliced
6 ripe tomatoes
2 tbsp red wine vinegar
3 tbsp olive oil
60g (2¼oz) wild rocket
20g (¾oz) mint
sea salt and pepper

1 Mix together the flour, oregano, rosemary, salt, pepper and cayenne.
Lightly dust the lamb leg steaks in the flour mixture. Cook over a barbecue,
or in a lightly oiled very hot griddle pan, for 3–5 minutes on each side until
nicely browned but still slightly pink in the centre.
2 To make the salad, combine the cucumber and red onion in a large serving
bowl. Halve each tomato horizontally, then cut each half into four. Add to the
bowl with the vinegar, olive oil and rocket. Tear in the mint leaves and
season with salt and pepper to taste. Toss gently together.
3 Place the lamb steaks on serving plates. Place the salad and a pile of warm
pitta breads or flour tortillas on the table so everyone can help themselves.

I can't tell you how many times I've made this,
but on warm, summer evenings when the
aromas of rosemary and mint start filling the
garden, it's the first choice for the barbecue.

Vietnamese beef noodles

Illustrated on previous pages

Serves 4

3 x 150g packets vacuum-packed
   straight-to-wok thin noodles
200g (7oz) mixed baby corn and
   mangetout
200g (7oz) small pak choi
1.2 litres (2 pints) hot chicken stock
4cm (1½ inch) piece fresh root
   ginger, peeled and cut into
   matchsticks

350g (12oz) very thin steaks
   (sandwich or minute steaks)
1 tbsp chilli sauce
2–3 tbsp soy sauce
juice of 2 limes, or to taste
150g (5oz) bean sprouts
handful of coriander leaves

1 Place the noodles in a heatproof bowl and pour over boiling water to cover.
Set aside.

2 Halve the baby corn and pak choi lengthways. Pour the stock into a large
pan, add the ginger and bring to the boil.

3 Meanwhile, heat a non-stick griddle pan until very hot. Brush the steaks
with the chilli sauce, then place them on the hot griddle pan and cook for
1 minute on each side. Transfer to a plate and set aside to rest for a couple
of minutes.

4 Add the baby corn, mangetout and pak choi to the stock, return to a
simmer and cook for about 2 minutes until just tender. Stir in the soy sauce
and lime juice to taste.

5 Drain the noodles and divide among four warm bowls. Add the bean
sprouts and ladle the stock on top. Thinly slice the steaks and add to the
bowls. Scatter coriander leaves over and serve.

This is a modern twist on classic Vietnamese street food, with a clean-flavoured, citrusy stock and lots of crunchy vegetables. It's one of my all-time favourite quick suppers.

Dill pickle cheese burgers

Serves 6

2 slices of white bread, crusts
   removed
20g (¾oz) flat leaf parsley, roughly
   chopped
1 egg
750g (1lb 10oz) lean beef mince
2 dill pickles, finely chopped, or
   2 tbsp chopped gherkins
sea salt and pepper

To serve

6 crusty buns, or burger buns
6 slices Port Salut, Jarlsberg or
   Cheddar cheese
tomato ketchup to taste (optional)

1 Tear the bread into pieces and place in a food processor with the parsley. Whiz until the bread is broken into crumbs. Transfer to a large bowl.
2 Using a wooden spoon, mix in the egg, beef, pickles and plenty of salt and pepper. You may need to use your hands to work the mixture together.
3 Preheat a griddle pan or the grill. Shape the mixture into eight even-sized burgers that are no more than 1cm (½ inch) thick. Cook on the griddle pan, or under the grill, for 3–4 minutes on each side until nicely browned and cooked to your taste.
4 Split open the buns and place a burger on the bottom of each. Top with a slice of cheese and a squirt of tomato ketchup if you like, then put on the lid and serve with salad.

These lovely juicy burgers – flavoured with crunchy pickles and topped with melting cheese – are always popular. If you want to spice up the burgers, deseed one or two red chillies and whiz with the bread and parsley.

Stir-fried steak chilli

Serves 4

1 tbsp vegetable oil
500g (1lb 2oz) rump steak, cubed
1 bunch of spring onions, trimmed
  and thickly sliced
4 mild green chillies, deseeded and
  roughly chopped
1 tsp cumin seeds
1 tsp cayenne pepper or hot chilli
  powder
4 ripe tomatoes, roughly chopped
410g can cannellini beans, drained
1 tbsp fruity brown sauce
2 tbsp chopped flat leaf parsley
sea salt and pepper

To serve

150ml (¼ pint) soured cream
150ml (¼ pint) ready-made
  guacamole
175g (6oz) tortilla chips

1 Heat a wok, add the oil and when it is very hot, add the steak. Stir-fry for
2–3 minutes until starting to brown. Add the onions, chillies, cumin seeds
and cayenne and stir-fry for another 2 minutes.
2 Lower the heat and stir in the tomatoes, then cook over a high heat for a
couple of minutes until they begin to soften. Add the cannellini beans and
fruity sauce, and simmer gently for a further 5 minutes until piping hot.
Season with salt and pepper to taste, and stir in the parsley.
3 Serve the chilli with plain boiled rice and pass round the soured cream,
guacamole and tortilla chips.

This is a guaranteed winner in my house
and it's incredibly quick to make – about
15 minutes from shopping bag to table.

Pan-fried pork chops with spinach

Serves 4

4 pork chops, each about 175g (6oz)

4 long rosemary sprigs

1 tbsp olive oil

1kg (2¼lb) leaf spinach, washed

small knob of butter

1 garlic clove, peeled and thinly
 sliced

sea salt and pepper

1 Push a metal skewer horizontally through each chop and remove, then push the rosemary sprig through each hole. Rub the chops with olive oil and season with salt and pepper.

2 Preheat a non-stick frying pan, then add the chops and cook gently for 15–20 minutes until nicely browned and cooked through.

3 Meanwhile, cram the spinach into a large pan, cover with a tight-fitting lid and cook gently for 5 minutes until wilted. Tip into a colander and press with a wooden spoon to extract the excess water.

4 Transfer the pork chops to à warm plate and set aside in a warm spot to rest for 5 minutes.

5 Add the butter to the hot frying pan, then toss in the garlic and cook for a minute or so. Add the wilted spinach and some seasoning and cook gently for 4–5 minutes, stirring from time to time.

6 Serve the chops with the soft spinach, and with any juices from the pork spooned over. Mashed potato is the perfect accompaniment.

When it comes to pork, I always say, take it nice and slow. When I've rubbed the chops with oil and seasoning, I cook them gently until they're golden but still tender and moist.

Fusilli with cabbage and crispy bacon

Serves 4

500g (1lb 2oz) dried fusilli or other
  pasta shapes
½ Savoy cabbage, thinly sliced
6 rashers of dry-cured streaky bacon
2 tbsp olive oil
1 onion, peeled and finely chopped

2 garlic cloves, peeled and thinly
  sliced
2 red chillies, halved, deseeded and
  thinly sliced
6 tbsp freshly grated Parmesan
  cheese, plus extra to serve
sea salt and pepper

1 Cook the pasta in a large pan of boiling salted water according to the
packet instructions until al dente (tender, but firm to the bite). About
5 minutes before the pasta is due to finish cooking, add the sliced cabbage to
the pan.
2 Meanwhile, cut the bacon rashers across into 1cm (½ inch) strips. Heat the
olive oil in a frying pan, add the bacon and cook for 1–2 minutes. Add the
onion, garlic and chillies and cook for a further 5 minutes until the onion
has softened.
3 Drain the pasta and cabbage well and return to the pan. Season the bacon
mixture with a little salt and plenty of pepper, then stir into the pasta and
cabbage. Sprinkle in the Parmesan and toss together. Divide among warm
bowls and serve immediately, with more grated Parmesan for passing round.

This tasty, satisfying supper is a good choice
when you're feeling a bit strapped for cash.

Sausage piece penne

Serves 6

900g (2lb) Lincolnshire sausages, or
  other quality pork sausages
2 onions, peeled and chopped
4 garlic cloves, peeled and chopped
2 red chillies, deseeded and finely
  chopped
3 sage sprigs

2 x 400g cans chopped tomatoes
1 tsp soft brown sugar
500g (1lb 2oz) dried penne or other
  pasta shapes
sea salt and pepper
freshly grated Parmesan cheese,
  to serve

1 Cut the sausages into 2.5cm (1 inch) pieces. Heat a large sauté pan or flameproof casserole and cook the sausage pieces, turning, for 5 minutes until lightly browned.

2 Drain off the excess fat to leave just a thin coating in the pan, then add the onions and garlic. Cook for 10 minutes, stirring occasionally, until golden brown.

3 Stir in the chillies and sage and cook for 1 minute. Add the tomatoes with their juice, the sugar and some salt and pepper. Bring to the boil, then half-cover and simmer gently for 40 minutes until dark and a little pulpy.

4 Meanwhile, cook the pasta in a large pan of boiling salted water according to the packet instructions until al dente (tender, but firm to the bite). Drain well and return to the pan, then add the sausage sauce and toss to mix.

5 Divide the hot pasta among warm bowls. Serve with Parmesan and don't forget the pepper mill.

To turn this into a warming pasta bake, pile into an ovenproof dish, sprinkle with grated Parmesan and bake at 200°C (fan oven 180°C), gas mark 6 for 30 minutes until the top is crusty and golden brown.

Chorizo and cannellini bean soup

Serves 4

2 tbsp olive oil
2 garlic cloves, peeled and chopped
1 onion, peeled and chopped
500g (1lb 2oz) floury potatoes, such
  as Maris Piper or King Edward,
  peeled and diced
2 tsp smoked paprika
1 litre (1¾ pints) hot vegetable stock
250g (9oz) chorizo sausage, roughly
  diced
410g can cannellini beans, drained
sea salt and pepper
2 tbsp chopped parsley, to serve

1 Heat the olive oil in a large saucepan. Add the garlic, onion and potatoes, and cook gently for about 10 minutes until golden. Stir in the paprika and stock and bring to the boil. Lower the heat and simmer for 15 minutes.
2 Stir in the chorizo sausage and cannellini beans and cook for 5 minutes or so, until piping hot. Season with a little salt and plenty of black pepper, then ladle into warm bowls and serve sprinkled with the chopped parsley.

Chorizo sausage has a wonderful smoky flavour, which gives this hearty soup a real blast of Spanish sunshine. The floury potato almost dissolves into the soup to give a lovely thick finish. Serve with warm crusty bread.

Butternut chowder with cheese toasties

Serves 4

2 tbsp olive oil
2 onions, peeled and finely chopped
2 garlic cloves, peeled and chopped
1kg (2¼lb) peeled butternut or
    kabocha squash flesh, cubed
1 litre (1¾ pints) hot vegetable stock
4 thyme sprigs
200ml (7fl oz) crème fraîche
sea salt and pepper

For the cheese toasties

40g (1½oz) easy-spread butter
8 slices of white bread
200g (7oz) Gruyère cheese, coarsely
    grated
20g (¾oz) chives or garlic chives,
    snipped

1 Heat the olive oil in a large saucepan and cook the onions, garlic and squash over a gentle heat for about 10 minutes until the onion has softened. Pour in the hot stock and stir in the thyme. Cover and simmer for about 30 minutes until the squash is tender.

2 Meanwhile, butter the bread. Make up four sandwiches with the cheese and chives, keeping the butter on the outside of the sandwiches. Preheat a griddle pan or large non-stick frying pan and cook the sandwiches, two at a time, for 2–3 minutes on each side until golden brown and the cheese is molten inside. Keep hot.

3 Remove the woody thyme stalks from the soup, then purée with a hand-held blender or in a blender goblet until smooth. Return to the pan if necessary. Stir in the crème fraîche and heat through gently without boiling. Check the seasoning.

4 Cut the toasties into squares or fingers. Ladle the soup into warm bowls and serve with the toasties.

Squash, such as butternut, cooks down to a wonderful velvety-textured soup. If possible, make it a day in advance – the flavours will really develop overnight in the fridge.

Lemony lentil and pasta soup

Serves 2

1 tbsp olive oil
1 onion, peeled and chopped
1 small garlic clove, peeled and
    finely chopped
1 carrot, peeled and chopped
400g can chopped tomatoes

50g (2oz) red lentils
900ml (1½ pints) vegetable stock
75g (3oz) dried fusilli or other
    pasta shapes
lemon juice, to taste
sea salt and pepper

1 Heat the olive oil in a pan and fry the onion, garlic and carrot for a few minutes to soften.
2 Stir in the tomatoes with their juice, the red lentils and stock. Bring to the boil, lower the heat and simmer for 30 minutes until the lentils are tender.
3 Meanwhile, cook the pasta in a large pan of boiling salted water according to the packet instructions until al dente (tender, but firm to the bite).
4 Once the lentils are cooked, stir in the drained pasta and a good squeeze of lemon juice. Season to taste, ladle into warm bowls and serve.

This satisfying soup can be assembled entirely from storecupboard ingredients. Serve with warm bread for a winter lunch or supper.

Cheese and tomato macaroni

Illustrated on previous pages

Serves 4

250g (9oz) cherry tomatoes
1 tbsp olive oil
350g (12oz) dried macaroni
250g tub mascarpone cheese
1 tbsp Dijon mustard
300g (11oz) fontina cheese, coarsely
   grated
sea salt and pepper

1 Preheat the oven to 220°C (fan oven 200°C), gas mark 7. Place the cherry tomatoes in a 2 litre (3½ pint) ovenproof dish. Drizzle over the olive oil and season with salt and pepper, then roast for 15 minutes until the tomatoes have softened slightly and the skins have split.

2 In the meantime, add the macaroni to a large pan of boiling salted water and cook according to the packet instructions until al dente (tender, but firm to the bite).

3 In a bowl, combine the mascarpone, mustard and fontina cheese, stirring until evenly blended.

4 Drain the pasta and return to the pan. Stir in the cheese mixture, then the roasted tomatoes and season with salt and pepper to taste. Tip the mixture back into the ovenproof dish used for the tomatoes. Bake for 25–30 minutes until golden brown and bubbling. Leave to stand for a few minutes, then serve straight from the dish.

Everyone loves macaroni cheese and this is a fantastic version. It skips the hassle of making a cheese sauce and packs even more flavour with the addition of roasted sweet cherry tomatoes.

Garlic mushroom linguine

Serves 4

400g (14oz) dried linguine
50g (2oz) butter
2 tbsp olive oil
3 garlic cloves, peeled and chopped
500g (1lb 2oz) chestnut mushrooms,
 thickly sliced

juice of 1 lemon, or to taste
20g (¾oz) tarragon or parsley,
 chopped
sea salt and pepper
freshly grated Parmesan cheese,
 to serve

1 Cook the pasta in a large pan of boiling salted water according to the packet instructions until al dente (tender, but firm to the bite).
2 Meanwhile, heat the butter and olive oil in a large frying pan and fry the garlic for 1 minute. Add the mushrooms with lemon juice to taste and cook for 10 minutes, stirring only once or twice, until tender and golden brown. Season generously with salt and pepper.
3 Drain the pasta well and return to the pan. Add the mushrooms and herbs, toss well and serve, with Parmesan to pass round.

This easy pasta dish uses the classic pairing of garlic and mushrooms. Serve with a full-bodied Italian red wine and lots of Parmesan.

Caramelised pepper spaghetti

Serves 6

4 tbsp olive oil

3 red peppers, cored, deseeded and thinly sliced

3 yellow peppers, cored, deseeded and thinly sliced

1 large onion, peeled and thinly sliced

650g (1lb 7oz) dried spaghetti

2 garlic cloves, peeled and thinly sliced

1 tbsp balsamic vinegar

20g (¾oz) basil leaves

4 tbsp freshly grated Parmesan cheese

sea salt and pepper

1 Heat the olive oil in a large sauté pan and very gently cook the peppers and onion with some salt and pepper over a low heat for 40–45 minutes, stirring from time to time, until the peppers become very soft and the onion is dark golden.

2 About 10 minutes before the peppers will be ready, cook the spaghetti in a large pan of boiling salted water according to the packet instructions until al dente (tender, but firm to the bite). Stir the garlic into the peppers and cook for a few more minutes. Add the vinegar and check the seasoning.

3 Drain the pasta well and return to the pan. Tear in the basil, then add the pepper mixture and Parmesan. Toss well, then serve.

Peppers are often quickly stir-fried to be crunchy, but sometimes it's better to let gentle slow-cooking release their natural sweetness.

Pea, mascarpone and mint risotto

Serves 4

1 tbsp olive oil

1 large onion, peeled and chopped

2 garlic cloves, peeled and chopped

400g (14oz) carnaroli or other
risotto rice

3 rosemary sprigs

150ml (¼ pint) Italian dry white wine

1.2 litres (2 pints) hot vegetable
stock

250g (9oz) frozen garden peas

250g tub mascarpone cheese

4 tbsp roughly chopped mint

sea salt and pepper

2 tbsp freshly grated Parmesan
cheese, to serve

1 Heat the olive oil in a large heavy-based saucepan, add the onion and garlic and cook for about 5 minutes until the onion has softened.

2 Stir in the rice and rosemary, then add the wine and cook vigorously for 2–3 minutes until it has been absorbed. Pour in half of the stock and leave to cook for 10 minutes or until the stock has been absorbed, stirring from time to time.

3 Add the rest of the stock and continue to cook for a further 5 minutes, then add the peas. Cook for another 5 minutes, stirring occasionally, until all the liquid has been absorbed and the rice is tender. Season with salt and pepper to taste, and remove the woody rosemary stalks. Ripple through the mascarpone and mint.

4 Before the mascarpone has completely melted, divide the risotto among warm bowls and top each with a sprinkle of Parmesan and a good grinding of black pepper. Serve swiftly.

This is a lovely soft risotto that's brought to the table with the mascarpone just melting. You can make it with any type of risotto rice, but carnaroli is always my first choice.

Satay noodles

Serves 2

2 blocks of egg noodles, about
  125g (4oz)
1–2 tbsp sunflower oil
1 large red pepper, cored, deseeded
  and thinly sliced
200g carton coconut cream

50g packet salted or dry-roasted
  peanuts, roughly chopped
dash of soy sauce
squeeze of lime juice
chopped coriander leaves or sliced
  spring onions, to serve

1 Add the egg noodles to a saucepan of boiling water and cook until tender, about 3–4 minutes.
2 Meanwhile, heat a splash of sunflower oil in a wok and stir-fry the red pepper slices over a high heat for 2–3 minutes.
3 Drain the noodles and add to the wok with the coconut cream, peanuts, soy sauce and lime juice. Heat, stirring, until piping hot.
4 Divide among warm bowls and scatter over some chopped coriander or sliced spring onions to serve.

This tasty noodle dish – prepared from storecupboard ingredients – is ideal for an impromptu meal when the fridge is empty.

Cheesy bean hash

Serves 2

750g (1lb 10oz) floury potatoes, such
   as Maris Piper or King Edward,
   peeled and cubed
400g can baked beans
pinch of dried chilli flakes

1–2 tbsp sunflower oil
50g (2oz) Cheddar cheese, grated
sea salt and pepper
sweet chilli sauce or tomato ketchup,
   to serve

1 Boil the potatoes in a saucepan of lightly salted water for 15–20 minutes
until tender, then drain well. Using a fork, roughly mash the potatoes with
the baked beans and chilli flakes.
2 Heat a little sunflower oil in a large non-stick frying pan. Add the bean
and potato mash and cook over a low heat, without turning, for 15 minutes
until the bottom is crisp and golden.
3 Turn the hash over, roughly breaking it up, then leave to cook for another
15 minutes until the base is crisp.
4 Add the grated cheese and stir through the mixture, then divide between
warm bowls. Add a grinding of pepper and top with a dollop of sweet chilli
sauce or tomato ketchup to serve.

If your family like baked beans and mash they
will adore this satisfying supper, which relies
on flavourings you are likely to have to hand.

Roasted pepper pizzettes

Illustrated on previous pages

Serves 6

4 x 145g packets pizza dough mix
500ml (16fl oz) warm water
flour, to dust
450g (1lb) yellow cherry tomatoes
285g jar roasted peppers in olive oil,
  drained

300g (11oz) mozzarella cheese,
  drained
2 tbsp olive oil
sea salt and pepper
basil leaves, to garnish

1 Preheat the oven to 200°C (fan oven 180°C), gas mark 6. Empty the pizza
dough mix into a bowl, make a well in the centre and pour in the warm
water. Mix according to the packet instructions, to make a soft dough.
Knead vigorously on a lightly floured surface for 5 minutes until smooth.
2 Divide the dough into six even-sized balls and roll out each roughly to a
20cm (8 inch) round. Transfer the rounds to two non-stick baking sheets and
leave to rise for 10 minutes.
3 Meanwhile, halve the cherry tomatoes, cut the peppers into strips and dice
the mozzarella. Arrange on top of the pizzas, drizzle over the olive oil and
season with salt and pepper. Bake for 20 minutes until risen and golden
brown. Tear the basil leaves over the pizzettes and serve immediately.

If there's a better time to make these than on a
lazy sunny afternoon, then I've yet to find it.
The sweet, bursting cherry tomatoes and soft,
creamy mozzarella are irresistible.

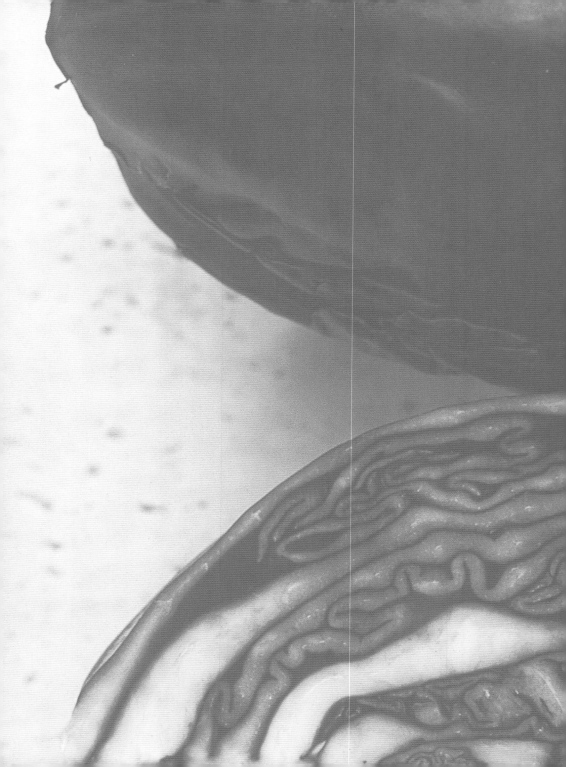

family
weekends

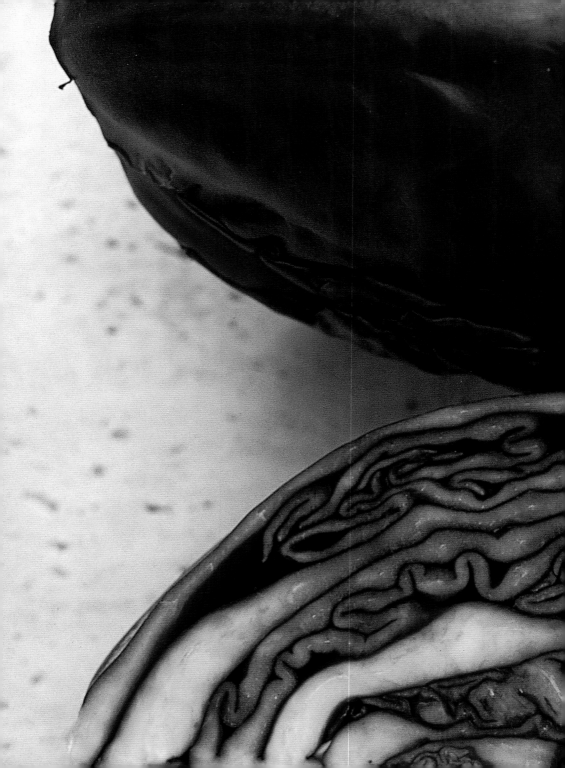

Pan-fried haloumi with fennel salad

Serves 6
2 small fennel bulbs
250g (9oz) haloumi cheese
seasoned flour, to dust
2–3 tbsp olive oil
sea salt and pepper

For the dressing
juice of 1 orange
4 tbsp olive oil
2 tbsp chopped mint or tarragon

1 Trim the fennel, reserving the feathery fronds for garnish. Using a swivel peeler, shave the fennel bulbs into wafer-thin slices and place in a bowl of chilled water. Cover and refrigerate for an hour to encourage the fennel shavings to curl and crisp.

2 To make the dressing, whisk the orange juice and olive oil together in a bowl. Season with salt and pepper and add the chopped mint or tarragon.

3 Drain the crisped fennel slices and pat dry on kitchen paper. Arrange on individual plates.

4 Cut the haloumi into 6 slices and dust with seasoned flour. Heat the olive oil in a frying pan and fry the haloumi slices for 2 minutes on each side until golden. Drain on kitchen paper.

5 Arrange the haloumi on the plates, garnish with the reserved fennel fronds and pour over the dressing. Serve swiftly.

For this easy starter, you can prepare the fennel and dressing ahead and simply deep-fry the haloumi slices just before serving.

Italian antipasti

Serves 6

200g (7oz) sliced cured meats, such as Italian salami, bresaola and Parma ham

150g (5oz) artichoke hearts in oil, drained and halved

150g (5oz) mixed black and green Italian olives

olive oil, to drizzle

small wedge of Parmesan cheese, freshly shaved

freshly ground black pepper

large wedge of dolcelatte cheese

To serve

breadsticks

rosemary and garlic focaccia

1 Arrange the sliced cured meats, artichoke hearts and olives on a serving platter. Drizzle with a little olive oil, shave over some Parmesan and finish with a good grinding of black pepper.

2 Place the wedge of dolcelatte on a board with a tumbler full of breadsticks. Pass around some warm rosemary and garlic focaccia.

Nothing could be simpler than this classic Italian starter, which leaves you plenty of time to concentrate on the main course – ideal if you are entertaining.

Courgette and mint soup

Serves 6
60g (2¼oz) butter
1 large onion, peeled and finely
    chopped
500g (1lb 2oz) courgettes, sliced
1.2 litres (2 pints) vegetable stock
large handful of chopped mint, plus
    extra to garnish
sea salt and pepper
100ml (3½fl oz) crème fraîche,
    to serve

1 Heat the butter in a large saucepan and fry the onion for 5–7 minutes
until softened. Add the sliced courgettes and cook, turning, for 2–3 minutes.
2 Pour in the vegetable stock and bring to a simmer. Season with salt and
pepper, cover and simmer for 10–15 minutes until the courgettes are tender.
3 Stir in a good handful of chopped mint, allow to cool slightly, then tip into
a blender and whiz until smooth.
4 To serve, heat through gently and pour into warm bowls. Top with the
crème fraîche and scatter over a little extra chopped mint.

A fresh-tasting soup is a great choice for a
starter and this one can be prepared well
ahead and frozen. Simply thaw overnight in
the fridge and reheat to serve.

Chilled fire soup shots

Serves 6

1 cucumber, peeled and roughly
   chopped
1kg (2¼lb) tomatoes, roughly
   chopped
2 red chillies, chopped
juice of 1 lime
sea salt and pepper
finely chopped coriander, to serve

1 Put the cucumber, tomatoes, chillies, lime juice and some salt into a food processor and whiz until well blended and slushy.

2 Pour into a muslin-lined large sieve set over a bowl and leave to drip through for several hours – don't force the juice through otherwise it will turn cloudy.

3 When the juice has dripped through, cover the bowl with cling film and chill until required.

4 When ready to serve, check the seasoning and stir in a little finely chopped coriander. Serve in shot glasses.

A fiery, chilled clear soup that is conveniently prepared ahead and elegantly served in little shot glasses as a starter.

Salmon pâté

Serves 6

125g packet roasted salmon
200g (7oz) soft cream cheese
½ tsp creamed horseradish
small handful of chopped chives
squeeze of lemon juice
sea salt and pepper

1 Flake the cooked salmon into a bowl and mix in the soft cheese, creamed horseradish, chopped chives and a squeeze of lemon juice. Season with salt and pepper to taste.
2 Serve the pâté with triangles of warm toast.

An incredibly easy starter, which can be prepared in a matter of minutes.

Spanish prawn soup

Serves 6

750g (1lb 10oz) raw prawns (any
    size will do), thawed if frozen
large knob of butter
2 shallots, peeled and sliced
2 garlic cloves, peeled and sliced
2 ripe tomatoes, roughly chopped

1 rosemary sprig
1 tbsp smoked paprika
pinch of dried chilli flakes
150ml (¼ pint) dry white wine
75g (3oz) short-grain rice, such as
    paella or risotto rice
sea salt and pepper

1 Peel the prawns and set aside, reserving the shells. Heat the butter in a
large pan and cook the shallots and garlic for 2 minutes. Add the prawn
shells and cook for a further 3–4 minutes.

2 Stir in the tomatoes, rosemary, paprika and chilli flakes and cook for
1 minute. Add the wine and cook vigorously for a couple of minutes, then
add 2 litres (3½ pints) water. Bring to the boil, cover and simmer gently for
20 minutes.

3 Strain the stock into a clean pan, then stir in the rice and some salt and
pepper. Bring to a gentle boil and simmer for 30 minutes until the rice is
very soft.

4 Add the prawns and cook for 3–5 minutes, depending on the size, until
they are pink. Whiz until smooth using a hand-held blender, or whiz in a
blender goblet and then reheat gently. Ladle into warm bowls and serve with
warm crusty bread.

This is my take on a classic bisque. The
addition of paprika and paella rice give the
soup an inviting Spanish flavour.

Smoked haddock and prawn pie

Serves 8

2kg (4⅓lb) floury potatoes, such as
   Maris Piper or King Edward,
   peeled and cubed
1 litre (1¾ pints) milk
750g (1lb 10oz) smoked haddock
   fillets
100g (3½oz) butter

75g (3oz) plain flour
100g (3½oz) Cheddar cheese, grated
300ml (½ pint) soured cream
150g (5oz) frozen peas, thawed
400g (14oz) peeled raw tiger prawns,
   thawed if frozen
20g (¾oz) chives, snipped
sea salt and pepper

1 Cook the potatoes in a large pan of boiling salted water for 15–20 minutes
until tender.

2 Meanwhile, pour the milk into a sauté pan and add the smoked haddock.
Bring gently to the boil, then remove from the heat and leave to stand for
5 minutes. Using a slotted spoon, transfer the smoked haddock to a plate
and set aside. Measure out 200ml (7fl oz) of the milk for the mash; the rest
will be used in the sauce.

3 To make the sauce, melt 75g (3oz) of the butter in a heavy-based pan. Stir
in the flour and cook for 1 minute. Gradually whisk in the milk for the
sauce. Bring to the boil, stirring, then simmer gently for 3–4 minutes.

4 Preheat the oven to 200°C (fan oven 180°C), gas mark 6. Drain the potatoes
and mash well. Stir in the milk reserved for the mash, the remaining butter,
the cheese and some seasoning.

5 Stir the soured cream and peas into the sauce together with the prawns
and heat gently for a couple of minutes without boiling. Pour into a deep
ovenproof dish. Stir in the chives. Flake in the haddock, discarding any
skin, and season to taste.

6 Spoon the mash over the top to cover the filling and rough up the surface,
using a fork. Place the dish on a baking sheet and bake for 30 minutes until
bubbling around the edges and golden brown.

Peking duck noodles

Illustrated on previous pages

Serves 6

1 plump duck, about 2kg (4½lb)
1 tbsp dark muscovado sugar
2 tsp sea salt
3 x 150g packets vacuum-packed
straight-to-wok noodles
1 tbsp sunflower oil
4cm (1⅓ inch) piece fresh root
ginger, peeled and diced
1 vegetable stock cube

1 tbsp cornflour, mixed with a
little water
2 tbsp sweet chilli sauce
1 tbsp soy sauce
4 Chinese leaves, shredded
1 red chilli, deseeded and finely
chopped
4 spring onions, thinly sliced
small handful of basil leaves,
to serve

1 Pierce the duck in several places with a skewer. Place on a rack over a roasting tin and pour over a kettle of boiling water. Drain off the water and pat the duck dry with kitchen paper, then put back on the rack. Mix the sugar and salt and rub into the duck skin. Leave in a cool, dry place for 2 hours.

2 Preheat the oven to 200°C (fan oven 180°C), gas mark 6. Pat the duck dry again, then roast for 1½ hours, basting from time to time, until the skin is crisp and dark and the meat is cooked through – pierce the thigh to check that it's not at all pink. Leave to rest for 10 minutes.

3 Meanwhile, put the noodles in a bowl, cover with boiling water and leave for 2–3 minutes, then drain. Heat a wok, add the oil and, when hot, add the noodles and ginger. Cook for 3 minutes without stirring so the noodles on the base crisp. Dissolve the stock cube in 300ml (½ pint) boiling water.

4 Stir to break up the noodles. Add the stock, cornflour, chilli and soy sauces, Chinese leaves, chilli and spring onions and stir-fry for 2–3 minutes. Using a cleaver or strong knife, cut the duck into pieces. Divide the noodle mixture among warm plates and top with the duck. Serve scattered with basil leaves.

Peking duck does take a bit of preparation
time, but my version is much simpler than the
classic Chinese method and worth the effort. It
makes an impressive dinner party dish too.

Chunky chicken and potato pie

Serves 6

1 tbsp olive oil

9 large skinless chicken thigh fillets, trimmed and quartered

2 potatoes, peeled and cut into 2cm (¾ inch) dice

1 red onion, peeled and cut into wedges

2 medium leeks, trimmed and thickly sliced

3 garlic cloves, peeled and halved

1 bay leaf

1 tbsp plain flour

50g (2oz) frozen peas

150ml (¼ pint) crème fraîche

150ml (¼ pint) chicken stock

small bunch of flat leaf parsley, roughly chopped

375g packet puff pastry, thawed if frozen

1 egg, beaten, to glaze

sea salt and pepper

1 Preheat the oven to 190°C (fan oven 170°C), gas mark 5. Put the olive oil in a small roasting tin or a large pie dish and add the chicken, potatoes, red onion, leeks, garlic cloves, bay leaf and flour. Toss well together, then season with salt and pepper. Roast for 25–30 minutes until tender, turning the chicken and vegetables occasionally.

2 Add the frozen peas, then stir in the crème fraîche, chicken stock and parsley. If you have time, leave the filling to cool.

3 Roll out the pastry until 2.5cm (1 inch) larger all round than the size of the roasting tin or pie dish. Lay the pastry over the filling, tucking in the edges down the sides of the tin, or pressing them on to the rim of pie dish (first brushing the rim with a little water).

4 Brush the top of the pie with beaten egg to glaze, then bake in the oven for 25–30 minutes until the pastry is risen and golden. Serve hot.

This pie has a delicious creamy flavour. It freezes very well, but make sure you allow plenty of time for it to thaw in the fridge.

Lemon chicken with sweet potato mash

Serves 6

2 free-range chickens, each about
   1.5kg (3¼lb), each cut into 8 pieces
12 garlic cloves
8 thyme sprigs
8 small preserved or pickled lemons,
   halved
25g (1oz) butter
sea salt and pepper

For the mash

2kg (4½lb) sweet potatoes, peeled
   and thickly sliced
1 tbsp olive oil
1 tbsp chopped rosemary
5–6 tbsp crème fraîche

1 Preheat the oven to 200°C (fan oven 180°C), gas mark 6. Pack the chicken pieces, garlic, thyme and lemons snugly in a large roasting tin. Season generously with salt and pepper, then dot over the butter. Roast for about 40 minutes until golden brown and cooked through.

2 Meanwhile, put the sweet potato slices in another roasting tin and stir in the olive oil, rosemary and some salt and pepper. Roast for 30 minutes until tender and golden. Roughly mash the sweet potatoes in the tin, then stir in the crème fraîche using a wooden spoon.

3 Divide the chicken among warm plates, making sure everyone gets some garlic and preserved lemon. Serve the sweet potato mash on the side.

Preserved lemons lend a Middle Eastern flavour to roast chicken, and creamy roast sweet potato purée is a great accompaniment.

Lamb and red cabbage hotpot

Illustrated on previous pages

Serves 6

2–3 tbsp vegetable oil

1.5kg (3¼lb) boneless shoulder of lamb, trimmed of excess fat and cut into large cubes

2 tbsp plain flour

1 large onion, peeled and sliced

4 garlic cloves, peeled and thinly sliced

6 thyme sprigs

1 small red cabbage, about 500g (1lb 2oz), cored and thinly sliced

150ml (¼ pint) ruby port

750ml (1¼ pints) lamb stock

4 tsp balsamic vinegar

1kg (2¼lb) red skinned potatoes, such as Desirée

25g (1oz) butter, melted

sea salt and pepper

1 Heat the oil in a large flameproof casserole. Dust the lamb with the flour and fry in batches for 3–4 minutes, stirring, until nicely browned all over.
2 Once all the meat is browned and set aside on a plate, add the onion to the casserole and cook for 5–8 minutes until soft and golden. Add the garlic and thyme and cook for a further minute or so.
3 Return the lamb to the pan, along with any juices on the plate. Stir in the cabbage, port, stock and vinegar. Bring to the boil, cover and simmer gently for 1–1½ hours until the lamb is very tender.
4 Meanwhile, preheat the oven to 200°C (fan oven 180°C), gas mark 6. Cook the potatoes in boiling salted water for 15 minutes. Drain and thickly slice.
5 Uncover the casserole and arrange the sliced potatoes over the lamb and and cabbage. Brush the potatoes with the melted butter and bake, uncovered, for 30 minutes until they are golden brown. Serve from the casserole.

This is the perfect comfort food for a cold winter's evening. I've used a boned shoulder of lamb, but you could use neck fillet or boned leg if you prefer.

Slow-roast leg of lamb in wine

Serves 6

2 tbsp olive oil

1 leg of lamb, about 2kg (4½lb)

2 tbsp plain flour

2 onions, peeled and thinly sliced

4 garlic cloves, peeled and thinly sliced

4 rosemary sprigs

2 x 75cl bottles dry white wine, or 1 bottle plus 750ml (1¼ pints) lamb stock

2 tbsp redcurrant jelly

sea salt and pepper

1 Preheat the oven to 170°C (fan oven 150°C), gas mark 3. Pour the olive oil into a large, sturdy roasting tin and set it on the hob to heat. Season the lamb, then roll it in the flour. Brown the lamb all over in the hot oil for 5–10 minutes.

2 Add the onions and cook for a further 5–10 minutes, turning the lamb and stirring the onions, until both are nicely browned. Add the garlic, rosemary, white wine (and stock if using) and redcurrant jelly. Bring to a simmer.

3 Transfer to the oven and cook for 3–3½ hours, basting the lamb now and again with the liquor. There should be a good quantity of liquor left in the bottom of the tin to serve with the lamb; if you feel it is getting too dry, just cover with foil.

4 Take the lamb out of the tin, place on a large warm platter and set aside to rest in a warm place. Meanwhile, put the tin back on the hob and simmer the pan juices for a few minutes, reducing the liquid if there is a lot, to make a tasty gravy.

5 Cut the lamb into thick slices – you'll find the meat falls away from the bone so you may end up with more chunks than slices. Serve with creamy mashed potatoes and the wine gravy.

Slow-cooking a leg of lamb in wine ensures it is meltingly tender and juicy. Rosemary adds flavour and fragrance and is balanced by a touch of sweetness from redcurrant jelly.

Meatball curry with chapattis and raita

Illustrated on previous pages

Serves 6
3 garlic cloves, peeled and quartered
2 red chillies, roughly chopped
1 thick slice of white bread, about
    50g (2oz)
1 tsp cumin seeds
4 tbsp mint leaves
750g (1lb 10oz) lean lamb mince
1 egg, beaten
1–2 tbsp vegetable oil
2 large onions, peeled and sliced
4 tomatoes, roughly chopped
500ml (16fl oz) hot lamb stock
3 tbsp hot curry paste
sea salt and pepper

For the raita
200g (7oz) Greek yogurt
1 small cucumber, peeled and
    roughly chopped
2 tbsp chopped mint
1 garlic clove, peeled and crushed
pinch of caster sugar
pinch of fine sea salt
squeeze of lemon juice

To serve
12 chapattis
25g (1oz) butter, melted
2 tsp ground coriander
small handful of mint leaves
1 lemon, cut into wedges

1 Put the garlic into a food processor with the chillies and tear in the bread. Add the cumin seeds and mint and pulse until finely chopped. Transfer to a bowl and stir in the minced lamb, beaten egg and plenty of salt and pepper. With damp hands, shape the mixture into walnut-sized balls.

2 Heat a splash of oil in a large non-stick sauté pan and fry the meatballs in batches over a high heat for 3–4 minutes until nicely browned; set aside. Add the onions to the pan and cook for 5–8 minutes until softened and golden. Add the tomatoes and cook for a further 2–3 minutes until pulpy.

3 Return the meatballs to the pan together with the lamb stock and curry paste. Stir gently, then bring to the boil and simmer gently for 30 minutes.

4 For the raita, combine the yogurt, cucumber, mint and garlic in a bowl, then stir in the sugar, salt and lemon juice to taste. Keep chilled.

5 When ready to serve, heat a griddle pan. Brush each chapatti with melted butter, sprinkle with ground coriander and cook on the hot griddle pan for 1 minute until speckled with brown. Divide the curry between warm bowls and scatter with mint. Serve with the raita, chapattis and lemon wedges.

Thick-crust beef and stout pie

Serves 8

2 tbsp olive oil

knob of butter

2 large onions, peeled and sliced

4 garlic cloves, peeled and chopped

4 tbsp plain flour

1.5kg (3¼lb) stewing or braising steak, cubed

2 x 500ml bottles chocolate stout or brown ale

3 tbsp soft brown sugar

2 thyme sprigs

sea salt and pepper

For the crust

75g (3oz) lard, diced

250g (9oz) plain flour

¼ tsp fine sea salt

1 egg, beaten, to glaze

1 Heat the olive oil and butter in a flameproof casserole and cook the onions and garlic for 5 minutes until softened. Meanwhile, season the flour with salt and pepper and use to dust the steak.

2 Using a slotted spoon, lift out the onions and reserve. Brown the steak in the casserole in two batches. Return all the meat and the onions to the casserole. Pour in the stout, then stir in the sugar, thyme and seasoning. Bring to the boil, partially cover and simmer very gently for 2 hours.

3 Preheat the oven to 200°C (fan oven 180°C), gas mark 6. To make the crust, heat the lard with 100ml (3½fl oz) water in a non-stick pan. Once boiling, shoot in the flour and salt, and stir with a wooden spoon until you have a smooth dough that forms a ball. Leave to cool for a few minutes.

4 Roll the dough out to a rough circle and use to cover the casserole. Brush the crust with the beaten egg and make a small hole in the middle to let the steam escape. Stand the casserole on a baking sheet. Bake for 30 minutes, then lower the oven temperature to 170°C (fan oven 150°C), gas mark 3 and bake for a further 1 hour until deep golden. Serve with mash.

This is a wonderful old-school steak pie with a delicious full flavour and a thick, firm pastry crust – arguably the best bit.

Boiled ham in fragrant broth with sticky rice

Serves 8

1 unsmoked prime gammon joint,
   about 2.2kg (4¾lb)
10cm (4 inch) piece fresh root
   ginger, roughly chopped
2 garlic cloves, peeled and roughly
   chopped

2 tomatoes, roughly chopped
1 bunch of spring onions
2 star anise
400g (14oz) sushi rice

1 Put the ham into a large pan with the ginger, garlic and tomatoes. Cut off and reserve the green part of the spring onions for serving. Slice the white part of the onions and add to the pan with the star anise. Cover with 3 litres (5 pints) cold water.

2 Bring to the boil, then partially cover the pan and simmer very gently for 3 hours, skimming the surface frequently. Towards the end of the time, cook the rice according to the packet instructions.

3 Carefully lift the ham on to a board, reserving the liquor, and leave to rest for a couple of minutes. In the meantime, finely slice the green spring onion. Carve the ham into slices.

4 Divide the rice among eight warm shallow bowls or soup plates and place the ham slices alongside. Strain the reserved liquor, then ladle some into each bowl and scatter with the spring onion (adding the star anise to a couple of bowls if you like). Serve swiftly.

An unusual twist on boiled ham, this is really fantastic. It is served with sticky rice and a ladleful of stock, although traditionalists can have their ham with mash if preferred.

Salt and pepper spare ribs

Serves 4

2 tbsp plain flour
1 tbsp Chinese five spice powder
½ tsp fine sea salt
½ tsp crushed black pepper
1kg (2¼lb) pork spare ribs
1 tbsp sunflower oil

1 bunch of spring onions, trimmed
   and thinly sliced
1 red chilli, deseeded and thinly
   sliced
1 garlic clove, peeled and finely
   chopped
2 tbsp soy sauce

1 Preheat the oven to 200°C (fan oven 180°C), gas mark 6. In a large bowl, mix together the flour, five spice powder, salt and pepper. Roll each rib in the seasoned flour, then place side by side on a rack over a roasting tin.
2 Roast for 40–50 minutes, turning from time to time, until cooked through and beautifully browned. Arrange the ribs on a large platter.
3 Heat a wok, then add the oil. When it is hot, add the spring onions and chilli and stir-fry over a high heat for 1 minute. Add the garlic and cook for a further 1 minute. Tip the contents of the wok over the ribs, then drizzle with the soy sauce. Serve immediately.

For the very popular oriental restaurant version of this dish, the spare ribs are usually deep-fried, but I prefer to roast them. Serve with noodles or a simple salad.

Aubergine, feta and broad bean salad

Serves 6

3 tbsp olive oil
4 large aubergines, cut into cubes
150g (5oz) podded fresh or frozen
  broad beans
1 large red onion, peeled and thinly
  sliced
juice of 1 lemon

3 tbsp avocado oil
250g (9oz) baby plum tomatoes,
  halved
1 garlic clove, peeled and crushed
2 tbsp chopped pitted black olives
2 tbsp finely chopped mint
2 x 200g (7oz) feta cheese, crumbled
sea salt and pepper

1 Preheat the oven to 220°C (fan oven 200°C), gas mark 7. Pour the olive oil into a shallow roasting tin and place in the oven to heat. Add the aubergine cubes, toss to coat in the hot oil and roast for 30 minutes, turning from time to time, until cooked through and golden brown.

2 Meanwhile, add the broad beans to a pan of boiling water, bring back to the boil and simmer for 2 minutes or until tender. Drain well and, once the beans are cool enough to handle, pop them out of their skins.

3 Tip the broad beans into a large bowl and add the red onion, lemon juice, 2 tbsp of the avocado oil and the tomatoes.

4 In another bowl, stir together the garlic, olives, mint and remaining avocado oil. Lightly fold in the crumbled feta and set aside.

5 Once the aubergine is cooked, tip it into the bowl of tomatoes and broad beans, and mix well. Season with salt and pepper to taste, then set aside for 5 minutes, or leave to cool to room temperature. Divide among plates and spoon over the feta mixture. Serve with warm pitta breads and a bowl of salad leaves as a summery lunch or supper.

Packed with Greek-style flavours, this salad always makes me think of the sun. The avocado oil imparts a wonderful flavour, but you can substitute olive oil if you prefer.

Taleggio and thyme risotto

Serves 6

50g (2oz) butter

1 red onion, peeled and finely chopped

2 garlic cloves, peeled and finely chopped

1 tsp thyme leaves

500g packet carnaroli risotto rice

300ml (½ pint) Italian dry white wine

1.2 litres (2 pints) hot vegetable stock

2 x 250g packets Taleggio cheese, roughly chopped

4 tbsp chopped parsley

sea salt and pepper

4 tbsp freshly grated Parmesan cheese, to serve

1 Heat the butter in a large pan and cook the onion with the garlic and thyme leaves for 5 minutes until softened and golden. Add the rice and stir to coat with the butter.

2 Pour in the wine and bubble vigorously for 5 minutes or so until the liquid has been absorbed. Gradually add the stock, roughly one-quarter at a time, stirring and simmering until each batch has been absorbed before adding the next. Total cooking time will be about 20 minutes.

3 Remove the risotto from the heat and stir through the Taleggio and parsley. Check the seasoning, adding salt and pepper to taste. Divide among warm serving bowls and top each with a sprinkling of Parmesan.

Risotto is a brilliant any-occasion dish. The addition of some soft, tasty Taleggio and fresh thyme makes this one rather special.

Red pepper and fontina cous cous cake

Serves 4

300g (11oz) cous cous
450ml (¾ pint) hot vegetable stock
juice of 1 lime
2 tbsp olive oil
½ x 280g jar roasted red peppers,
    drained and cut into 1cm (½ inch)
    wide strips

200g (7oz) fontina or Gruyère
    cheese, cut into small dice
1 egg, beaten
4 tbsp snipped chives
freshly ground black pepper

1 Put the cous cous into a large heatproof bowl. Stir together the vegetable stock, lime juice and a good grinding of black pepper, then pour over the cous cous. Leave for 15 minutes until all the stock has been absorbed.

2 Heat a splash of the olive oil in a 23cm (9 inch) non-stick frying pan. Stir the peppers, cheese, egg and chives into the cous cous, then tip into the pan and pat down well into a cake. Cook over a gentle heat for 15 minutes, without touching, until the base is crisp and golden.

3 Carefully slide the cous cous cake on to a plate, then invert back into the pan, adding the rest of the oil if needed. Cook for a further 10 minutes or so until the other side is golden. Slide the cous cous cake back on to the plate and cut into wedges to serve.

This makes a lovely light lunch – perfect with a rocket and tomato salad. To ensure the cous cous holds together, it must be slightly over-moistened, which is why there is more stock than usual.

Cheese and onion baked potatoes

Ge

Serves 6

6 baking potatoes, each about 250g (9oz)

1 tbsp olive oil

coarse sea salt, to sprinkle

2 small red onions, peeled and very finely chopped

75g (3oz) Gruyère or Emmental cheese, grated

75g (3oz) mature Cheddar cheese, grated

300ml (½ pint) soured cream

sea salt and pepper

1 Preheat the oven to 200°C (fan oven 180°C), gas mark 6. Pierce each potato in several places with a fork, then rub with the olive oil and sprinkle with salt. Bake directly on the middle oven shelf for 1 hour and 20 minutes, turning from time to time.

2 To check that the potatoes are cooked, wrap them in a clean tea towel and give them a gentle squeeze – they should feel soft. Keeping each potato wrapped in the tea towel, hit each one with your fist, so that the skin splits (this looks more natural than cutting them open).

3 Scoop the fluffy flesh out of the potatoes and place in a bowl. Stir in the onions, grated cheeses, soured cream and some salt and pepper. Roughly pile the mixture back into the potato shells. Place on a baking sheet and bake for 30–40 minutes until golden brown. Serve hot, with salad or baked beans.

These are the most delicious jacket potatoes I have ever eaten. I keep the red onions raw, as I like the freshness they offer, but soften them first in a little olive oil if you prefer.

family
lunchboxes
and
snacks

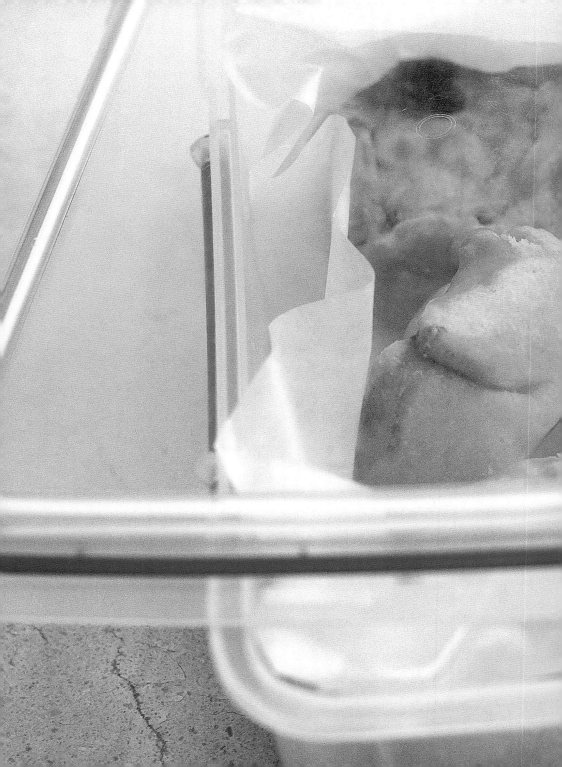

Sticky lemon chicken wings

Serves 4
12 large chicken wings
25g (1oz) butter, melted
grated zest and juice of 1 lemon
1 tsp chilli powder
¼ tsp sea salt

1 Preheat the oven to 200°C (fan oven 180°C), gas mark 6. Using a strong pair of scissors, snip the tip off each wing and discard.
2 In a small bowl, mix together the melted butter, lemon zest and juice, chilli powder and salt.
3 Arrange the chicken wings on a rack set over a baking tray and brush both sides with the lemony butter. Roast for 30–40 minutes, turning and basting once or twice, until golden brown.

Easy and delicious, baked chicken wings are the ideal late-night snack, eaten hot from the oven. Or you can eat them cold the next day, packed in a lunchbox or picnic basket.

Parma ham and mozzarella focaccia

Illustrated on previous pages

Serves 6

250g (9oz) floury potatoes, such as
 Maris Piper or King Edward,
 peeled and cubed
1kg (2¼lb) Italian '0' flour, or
 strong white bread flour, plus
 extra to dust
7g sachet fast-action dried yeast
2 x 85g packets sliced Parma ham,
 roughly torn
300g (11oz) mozzarella cheese,
 drained and diced
6 sun-dried tomatoes in oil, drained
 and diced
1 tsp fine salt
2 tbsp olive oil
2 tbsp Italian or French chilli oil
 (not oriental style)
1 tsp coarse sea salt
1 rosemary sprig, roughly chopped

1 Cook the potatoes in a large pan of boiling salted water for 15 minutes
until tender. Drain well and turn into a large bowl. Mash thoroughly, then
leave to cool.

2 Tip the mash on to a lightly floured surface and add the flour, yeast, ham,
mozzarella, sun-dried tomatoes and fine salt. Make a well in the centre and
add the olive oil and 400ml (14fl oz) warm water. Gradually incorporate the
dry ingredients into the liquid and mix to a soft dough, adding a little warm
water if needed.

3 Knead the dough on a floured surface for a good 5 minutes until smooth.
Roll out to a large oval shape, about 1cm (½ inch) thick. Transfer to a baking
sheet, cover with a clean tea towel and leave to rise for an hour or so until
doubled in size.

4 Preheat the oven to 200°C (fan oven 180°C), gas mark 6. Using your
fingertips, make indentations about 2cm (¾ inch) deep all over the surface of
the dough. Drizzle with the chilli oil and sprinkle with sea salt and
rosemary. Bake for 35–40 minutes until risen and golden brown. Allow to
cool for a few minutes before slicing.

Here a classic focaccia dough is reinforced
with potato to give a gorgeous texture that
really satisfies. Cut into wedges and eat in
place of a regular sandwich.

Chicken palm pies

Also illustrated on previous pages

Makes 12

75g (3oz) cubed pancetta, or dry-
   cured streaky bacon, cut into
   small strips
4 large skinless chicken thigh fillets
1 tsp cornflour
1 small onion, peeled and finely
   chopped

1 tsp chopped sage
100ml (3½fl oz) chicken stock
squeeze of lemon juice
500g (1lb 2oz) ready-made
   shortcrust pastry
1 egg yolk
sea salt and pepper

1 Cook the pancetta or bacon in a large non-stick frying pan for 3–4 minutes
until crisp and golden brown. Remove with a slotted spoon and set aside.
2 Cut the chicken thighs into 1cm (½ inch) pieces and dust with the
cornflour. Add to the frying pan with the onion and cook for 8–10 minutes
until well browned and cooked through, adding the sage for the last minute
of the cooking time.
3 Stir in the stock and bring to the boil. Season with salt and pepper and add
a squeeze of lemon juice to taste, then leave to cool.
4 Preheat the oven to 200°C (fan oven 180°C), gas mark 6. Roll out three-
quarters of the pastry, stamp out twelve 15cm (6 inch) discs and use to line a
12-hole muffin tin, allowing excess pastry to overhang the edges. Roll out
the remaining pastry and stamp out twelve 7.5cm (3 inch) discs for lids.
5 Stir the pancetta or bacon into the chicken mixture, then divide among the
pastry cases. Dampen the inside edges of the pastry cases with a little water.
Lay the pastry lids on top of the filling, then fold the edges of the pastry
case over and press together to seal. Cut a small hole in the top of each pie.
6 Mix together the egg yolk and ¼ tsp salt. Brush over the pies, then bake
for 20 minutes until the pastry is crisp and well glazed. Leave to cool. Wrap
individually in waxed or greaseproof paper to pack into lunchboxes.

These lovely little pies are so named because
they fit in the palm of your hand. They are
perfect for lunchboxes, and ideal for freezing.

Skewered lamb and aubergine pittas

Serves 2
¼ cucumber, roughly chopped
2 tomatoes, roughly chopped
handful of chopped mint
squeeze of lemon juice
olive oil, to drizzle
2 pitta breads
4 tbsp ready-made aubergine dip
2 ready-cooked lamb skewers
sea salt and pepper

1 Combine the chopped cucumber, tomatoes and mint in a bowl. Squeeze over a little lemon juice, add a drizzle of olive oil and season well with salt and pepper.
2 Toast the pitta breads in the toaster or under a hot grill. Split them open and spoon 2 tbsp aubergine dip into each one.
3 Slide the meat from the lamb skewers into each pitta and spoon in the tomato and cucumber salad. Wrap the pittas in foil and pack into lunchboxes.

Buy ready-made aubergine dip and cooked lamb skewers from the deli counter and pack into pittas with a minted cucumber and tomato salad for a tempting packed lunch.

Chicken tikka wraps

Serves 4

4 small skinless chicken breast
  fillets
150g (5oz) natural yogurt
1 garlic clove, peeled and crushed
1 tsp ground cumin
¼ tsp cayenne pepper
¼ tsp ground turmeric
½ tsp sea salt
4 flour tortilla wraps, warmed
4–6 Iceberg lettuce leaves, shredded
lemon wedges, to serve

1 Preheat the grill. Cut the chicken breast fillets into 1cm (½ inch) strips. In a bowl, mix the yogurt with the crushed garlic, cumin, cayenne, turmeric and salt. Add the chicken strips and toss to coat.
2 Place the chicken strips on the foil-lined grill pan and grill, turning occasionally, until evenly coloured and cooked through. Meanwhile, warm the tortilla wraps in the microwave or in a dry frying pan.
3 Divide the chicken between the warm tortilla wraps, scatter with shredded lettuce and roll up tightly, then wrap in greaseproof paper.
4 Serve the chicken tikka wraps with lemon wedges for squeezing.

There's no limit to the fillings that can go into tortilla wraps. Try grilled aubergine slices and crumbled feta, or sliced cold roast beef with peppery rocket and horseradish – delicious!

Ham and cheese puffs

Makes 4

375g packet ready-rolled puff pastry

1 tbsp Dijon mustard

200g (7oz) Gruyère, Emmental or
   Jarlsberg cheese, thinly sliced

50g (2oz) wafer-thin ham, roughly
   torn

25g (1oz) butter, melted

1 Preheat the oven to 200°C (fan oven 180°C), gas mark 6. Roll out the puff
pastry to a 30 x 46cm (12 x 18 inch) rectangle. Cut into eight 15 x 11cm
(6 x 4½ inch) rectangles.

2 Spread four of the rectangles with the mustard, then cover with the
cheese, taking the slices right up to the edges. Scatter over the torn ham.
Place the other four rectangles of puff pastry on top and press down firmly.
Squeeze the edges of each tart together between your thumb and forefinger
to seal them.

3 Arrange the tarts on a baking sheet lined with silicone paper and brush
them with melted butter. Bake for 20 minutes until dark golden. The cheese
will ooze out around the edges but don't worry.

4 Lift the tarts off the paper and cool slightly for a few minutes before
serving. Alternatively, allow to cool and reheat in the toaster.

These are best eaten hot, straight from the
oven. Alternatively, wrap them in greaseproof
paper and pop into your lunchbox.

Spicy omelette chapatti

Serves 1

1 tsp vegetable oil
1 green chilli, chopped
1 spring onion, trimmed and
  chopped
3 cherry tomatoes, halved
1 tsp garam masala
1 large egg, lightly beaten
1 chapatti
1 tbsp sweet chilli sauce

1 Heat the oil in a small frying pan, add the green chilli, spring onion and cherry tomatoes and cook gently for 2–3 minutes.

2 Stir in the garam masala and cook for 1 minute. Swirl in the beaten egg and cook until the base is set. Flip the omelette over and cook for a minute on the other side. Meanwhile, warm the chapatti in the microwave or in a dry frying pan.

3 Place the omelette on the chapatti and spoon the sweet chilli sauce on top. Roll up and serve warm, or wrap in greaseproof paper, then foil and pack into a lunchbox.

With a little imagination, flat breads, such as chapattis, tortilla wraps, pitta breads and Californian wraps, can be transformed into fabulous lunches and snacks.

Crusty Tex-Mex roll

Serves 1

1 crusty roll
3 tbsp canned refried beans
½ green chilli, finely chopped
handful of grated Cheddar cheese
1 tbsp soured cream

1 Slice the top off the crusty roll and set aside. Remove most of the bread from the inside, leaving a layer, about 1cm (½ inch) thick, inside the crust.
2 Mix the refried beans with the chopped green chilli and use to fill the roll. Top with the grated cheese and a dollop of soured cream.
3 Replace the crusty top and wrap the roll in cling film or waxed paper. Leave for an hour or so before eating.

I love the Mexican flavours in this satisfying roll. It is best prepared a while before eating, to allow the flavours to develop.

Potato pasties

Makes 10

750g (1lb 10oz) floury potatoes, such as Maris Piper or King Edward, peeled and cubed
1 tbsp olive oil
2 shallots, peeled and finely chopped
1 garlic clove, peeled and finely chopped
1 tsp cayenne pepper
1 tsp made English mustard
200g (7oz) Cheddar cheese, coarsely grated
200g (7oz) ready-made filo pastry (10 sheets)
25g (1oz) butter, melted
sea salt and pepper

1 Boil the potatoes in a pan of salted water for 15 minutes or until tender.
2 Meanwhile, heat the olive oil in a large non-stick frying pan and gently cook the shallots and garlic for 2–3 minutes. Drain the potatoes well and add to the frying pan, mashing them roughly with a fork. Leave to cool.
3 Preheat the oven to 200°C (fan oven 180°C), gas mark 6. Stir the cayenne, mustard and cheese into the potato mixture, seasoning generously with salt and pepper.
4 Cut each sheet of filo pastry in half lengthways to give twenty 30 x 9cm (12 x 3½ inch) strips. Place two strips of pastry on a surface, overlapping them at right angles to form an L shape. Spoon some of the potato mixture on to the overlapped corner, then fold over the two strips alternately to enclose the filling. Turn over, then fold the two strips back over so that you make a square parcel with all four sides enclosed.
5 Brush lightly with melted butter and transfer to a non-stick baking sheet. Bake for 20 minutes until crisp and golden brown. Serve warm, or cool on a wire rack before wrapping in greaseproof paper or foil.

A box of filo pastry makes a lot of pasties, which is terrific as they freeze brilliantly – simply pack them in pairs in small bags. Once thawed you can warm them up in the oven.

Butternut squash and Parmesan muffins

Makes 12

1 small butternut squash, about 400g (14oz), peeled, deseeded and diced

1 red onion, peeled and finely chopped

1 tbsp olive oil

75g (3oz) butter, melted

150g (5oz) Parmesan cheese, freshly grated, plus a little extra to sprinkle

225g (8oz) self-raising flour

4 eggs, beaten

3–4 tbsp milk

sea salt and pepper

1 Preheat the oven to 200°C (fan oven 180°C), gas mark 6. Place the squash and onion on a baking sheet and drizzle over the olive oil. Season with salt and pepper and bake for 15 minutes until tender. Roughly mash on the baking sheet.

2 Lower the oven temperature to 180°C (fan oven 160°C), gas mark 4. Line a 12-hole muffin tin with squares of greaseproof paper (pushed in roughly) or with paper cases.

3 Spoon the pumpkin and onion mixture into a large bowl and stir in the melted butter, Parmesan, flour, eggs, milk and some salt and pepper to make a thick, lumpy batter. Divide the mixture among the cases and sprinkle over some extra Parmesan. Bake for 20–25 minutes until golden and just firm.

4 Transfer to a wire rack to cool. Serve warm or cool completely before packing into lunchboxes.

The combination of butternut squash and Parmesan not only tastes delicious but also makes these easy muffins nutritious and satisfying. Eat within a day of baking.

Sesame chicken noodle salad

Serves 2

75g (3oz) flat rice noodles
175g (6oz) cooked chicken breast
1 tbsp soy sauce
2 tbsp sweet chilli sauce
4 spring onions, trimmed and finely
  chopped

2 tsp sesame seeds, toasted
½ tsp toasted sesame oil
handful of coriander leaves,
  roughly torn
sea salt and pepper

1 Put the rice noodles into a heatproof bowl. Pour on boiling water to cover generously and leave to soak for 5 minutes.
2 Meanwhile, remove the skin from the chicken and cut the flesh into fine strips. Place in a bowl, add the soy sauce and chilli sauce, and toss to mix.
3 Drain the rice noodles, refresh under cold running water and drain thoroughly. Add to the chicken strips with the spring onions, sesame seeds and sesame oil. Toss well and season with salt and pepper to taste. Add the coriander leaves.
4 Either serve at once or pack into plastic tubs for lunchboxes.

This oriental-style salad is a tasty, satisfying alternative to a sandwich lunch. Either buy cooked chicken portions from the deli counter, or use chicken leftover from the Sunday roast.

Gorgeous cranberry cookies

Makes 24

175g (6oz) unsalted butter, at room temperature

150g (5oz) golden caster sugar

finely grated zest of 1 large orange

2 egg yolks

50g (2oz) ground almonds

50g (2oz) dried cranberries or cherries

225g (8oz) self-raising flour

2 tbsp milk

1 Preheat the oven to 170°C (fan oven 150°C), gas mark 3. Using an electric mixer, beat together the butter and sugar until pale and creamy.

2 Stir in the orange zest, egg yolks, ground almonds, dried cranberries and flour. Mix well together, then roll into walnut-sized balls.

3 Place on a baking sheet, spaced well apart, and flatten each ball slightly with your hand. Brush with milk, then bake for 18–20 minutes until golden.

4 After removing from the oven, leave the cookies to firm up on the baking sheet for 5 minutes before transferring to a wire rack to cool. Store in an airtight container.

These scrumptious cookies really deserve their name – they're crunchy with a lovely buttery flavour and little nuggets of chewy dried cranberry.

Caramel ripple brownies

Makes 16

100g (3½oz) luxury dark chocolate
100g (3½oz) unsalted butter
2 eggs, beaten
150g (5oz) light muscovado sugar
50g (2oz) plain flour

For the caramel ripple

200g (7oz) soft cheese
50g (2oz) dark muscovado sugar
few drops of vanilla extract
1 egg

1 Preheat the oven to 170°C (fan oven 150°C), gas mark 3. Line a 20cm
(8 inch) square shallow cake tin with silicone paper or baking parchment.
2 Break up the chocolate into a heatproof bowl and add the butter. Set over
a pan of gently simmering water and melt, stirring from time to time.
3 Meanwhile, prepare the caramel ripple mixture. Combine the soft cheese,
muscovado sugar, vanilla extract and egg in a bowl and mix well until
evenly blended. Set aside.
4 Stir the eggs and sugar into the chocolate mixture, then sift over the flour
and gently fold in.
5 Spoon half of the chocolate mixture into the prepared tin, then alternately
dollop teaspoonfuls of the caramel mixture and the remaining chocolate
mixture on top. Using a chopstick or skewer, lightly ripple together to make
a marbled top.
6 Bake for 25–30 minutes until just set. Leave to cool in the tin for
5–10 minutes before cutting into squares. Transfer the brownies to a wire
rack to cool completely.

These rich, rippled brownies are fantastic
served with coffee. As they are quite dense,
cut them into small squares and wrap in foil
for lunchboxes.

Lemon custard tarts

Illustrated on previous pages

Makes 24

350g packet puff pastry, thawed
   if frozen
1 vanilla pod
300ml (½ pint) milk
1 egg

1 egg yolk
50g (2oz) caster sugar
25g (1oz) plain flour
grated zest and juice of ½ lemon
icing sugar, to dust (optional)

1 Preheat the oven to 200°C (fan oven 180°C), gas mark 6. Roll out the pastry as thinly as possible, then stamp out 24 rounds, each 7cm (2¾ inches) in diameter. Use to line two 12-hole mini muffin tins.

2 Fill each pastry case with a dense ball of foil. Bake for 10–15 minutes until crisp and light golden, remove the foil and set aside. Lower the oven temperature to 170°C (fan oven 150°C), gas mark 3.

3 To make the filling, split the vanilla pod lengthways and place in a saucepan with the milk. Heat until almost boiling, then set aside for 10 minutes. Meanwhile, beat together the egg, egg yolk, sugar and flour in a bowl until smooth.

4 Remove the vanilla pod from the warm milk, then gradually pour on to the egg mixture. Return to a clean pan and stir over a medium heat until simmering. When the mixture begins to simmer, beat it quite vigorously to get rid of any lumps. Stir in the lemon zest and juice.

5 Divide the lemon filling among the pastry cases. Bake the tarts for 10–15 minutes until the custard filling has set. Leave in the tins for a few minutes, then carefully transfer to a wire rack to cool. Dust with icing sugar before serving if you like.

Based on fashionable Portuguese tarts, these yummy lemony mouthfuls, paired with a shot of hot black coffee, will really perk you up. Fortunately they are robust enough to tuck into school lunchboxes too.

Rough raspberry and almond slice

Serves 8

500g (1lb 2oz) ready-made
  shortcrust pastry
50g (2oz) butter, at room
  temperature
50g (2oz) golden caster sugar

1 small egg
125g (4oz) ground almonds
few drops of vanilla extract
125g (4oz) raspberries
25g (1oz) flaked almonds
1 tbsp icing sugar

1 Preheat the oven to 200°C (fan oven 180°C), gas mark 6. Roll out the pastry to a 30 x 20cm (12 x 8 inch) rectangle – don't worry if the edges aren't straight, as that's part of the charm. Transfer to a non-stick baking sheet and prick in several places. Bake for 5 minutes until set.

2 Meanwhile, using an electric mixer, beat the butter and caster sugar together until pale and fluffy. Stir in the egg, ground almonds and vanilla extract to make a stiff paste.

3 Spread the almond paste on top of the pastry, leaving a 1cm (½ inch) border clear on all sides. Gently press the raspberries into the paste. Scatter over the almonds and sift over the icing sugar. Bake for 20–25 minutes until puffed and golden.

4 Leave on the baking sheet for a few minutes, then carefully transfer to a wire rack to cool. Slice and serve warm, or at room temperature.

Here's a rustic version of a classic Bakewell tart. Having grown up in Derbyshire, I know the original (soggy) Bakewell pudding only too well – I would rather tuck into one of these slices any day!

Moist mango and maple cake

Serves 8

125g (4oz) butter
150g (5oz) light muscovado sugar
100g (3½oz) maple syrup
150g (5oz) plain flour
100g (3½oz) wholemeal flour
2 tsp baking powder
1 tbsp ground cinnamon
2 ripe mangoes, peeled, stoned and
  finely chopped
100g (3½oz) pecan nuts, roughly
  chopped

For the frosty topping

grated zest and juice of 1 small
  orange
200g (7oz) soft cheese
50g (2oz) icing sugar, sifted

1 Preheat the oven to 170°C (fan oven 150°C), gas mark 3. Gently melt the butter, sugar and maple syrup together in a small pan.

2 In a large bowl, mix together the flours, baking powder, cinnamon, mango and pecan pieces. Stir in the melted syrup mixture.

3 Spoon the mixture into a non-stick 500g (1lb) loaf tin – about 16 x 10cm and 8cm deep (6½ x 4 inches and 3¼ inches deep). Bake for 1–1¼ hours until a skewer inserted into the centre of the cake comes out clean.

4 Leave the cake to cool in the tin for 5 minutes, then turn out on to a wire rack to cool completely.

5 For the topping, mix together the orange zest, soft cheese and icing sugar with enough of the orange juice to make a smooth, thick paste. Spread thickly over the top of the cooled cake. Cut into slices to serve.

This loaf cake is reminiscent of a traditional carrot cake, so I've topped it with a cream cheese frosting. Wrap thick slices in waxed or greaseproof paper for picnics and lunchboxes.

family
just for
two

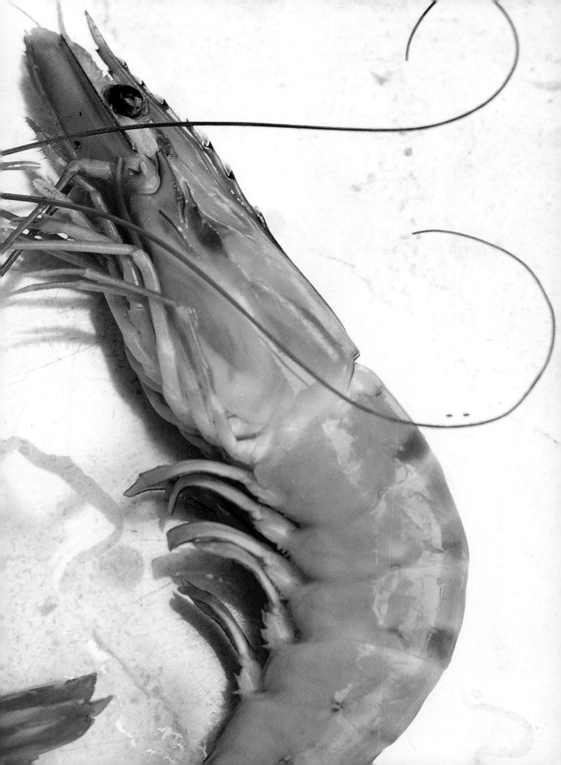

Tiger prawn tagliatelle

S͏͏e͏
1
1 garlic clove, peeled and thinly
   sliced
3 ripe tomatoes, chopped
grated zest of 1 small lemon
squeeze of lemon juice

pinch of sugar
pinch of dried chilli flakes
200g (7oz) cooked, peeled tiger
   prawns
250g (9oz) fresh tagliatelle
2 tbsp chopped flat leaf parsley
sea salt and pepper

1 Heat the olive oil in a small frying pan and cook the garlic for 1 minute until beginning to soften. Add the tomatoes and simmer gently for about 5 minutes until they become pulpy.

2 Add the lemon zest and lemon juice, together with the sugar, chilli flakes and seasoning to taste. Stir to mix. Add the cooked prawns and cook gently for a couple of minutes until heated through.

3 Meanwhile, cook the pasta in a large pan of boiling salted water according to the packet instructions until al dente (tender, but firm to the bite).

4 Drain the pasta well and return to the pan. Add the prawn sauce and parsley, toss to mix, then divide between warm bowls and serve.

This is the perfect choice for a romantic supper for two. I've used fresh tagliatelle here, but you could always use dried pasta – put it on to boil at the start and the sauce will be ready in the time it takes the pasta to cook.

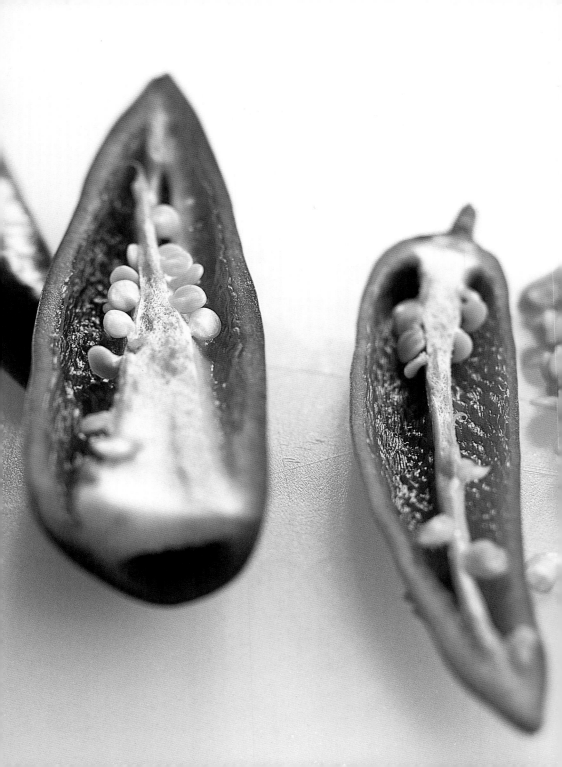

Griddled tuna with fiery tomato salsa

Illustrated on previous pages

Serves 2

2 ripe tomatoes, roughly chopped
1 shallot, peeled and thinly sliced
1 small garlic clove, peeled and
    very thinly sliced
1 green chilli, finely chopped
pinch of dried chilli flakes

juice of 1 lime
2 tbsp olive oil
2 fresh tuna steaks, each about
    175g (6oz)
1 tsp cracked black peppercorns
2 tbsp chopped mint or coriander
sea salt and pepper

1 Mix the tomatoes, shallot, garlic, fresh and dried chilli together in a bowl.
Stir in the lime juice, 1 tbsp olive oil and some salt and pepper. Set aside at
room temperature for at least 5 minutes, or up to an hour.
2 Preheat a ridged griddle pan. Rub the rest of the olive oil over the tuna
steaks. Sprinkle over the cracked peppercorns and press them in lightly with
your fingertips.
3 Cook the tuna for 2–3 minutes on each side until nicely browned but still
slightly pink in the centre. Place on two warm plates. Stir the mint into the
salsa, then spoon over and alongside the tuna.

Fresh tuna has a meaty texture and a mild
flavour that's well matched with a wicked little
salsa like this one. Serve with summer leaves
or crusty bread.

Quick coq au vin

Serves 4

2 tbsp olive oil

8 large chicken thighs

4 rashers of dry-cured streaky
bacon, chopped

8 shallots, peeled

225g (8oz) chestnut mushrooms,
halved

2 tbsp brandy

300ml (½ pint) red wine

200ml (7fl oz) chicken stock

2 tbsp tomato purée

1 bay leaf

sea salt and pepper

1 Heat the olive oil in a large sauté pan and fry the chicken thighs for
4 minutes on each side until golden. Remove from the pan and set aside.
2 Add the chopped bacon, shallots and chestnut mushrooms to the pan and
fry, stirring, for 5 minutes.
3 Return the chicken, then add the brandy and cook for 1 minute. Pour in
the red wine and chicken stock, stirring well, then add the tomato purée
and bay leaf. Season with salt and pepper and bring to a simmer.
4 Cover and simmer gently for 15 minutes, then cook, uncovered, for a
further 10 minutes or until the chicken is tender. Serve with mash.

This recipe freezes beautifully, so I have made
it to give you two meals for two – one to eat
now and one to freeze for later.

Potato stuffed poussins

Serves 2

1 large floury potato, such as Maris Piper or King Edward, about 225g (8oz), peeled and diced

1 tbsp olive oil

3 rosemary sprigs

1 garlic clove, peeled and finely chopped

1 shallot, peeled and sliced

pinch of dried chilli flakes

1 lemon

2 poussins, each about 500g (1lb 2oz)

25g (1oz) butter, at room temperature

sea salt and pepper

1 Boil the potato in a pan of salted water for 10–15 minutes until tender.

2 Preheat the oven to 200°C (fan oven 180°C), gas mark 6. Heat the oil in a small frying pan. Strip the leaves off one of the rosemary sprigs, roughly chop and add to the pan with the garlic and shallot. Cook for 5 minutes until softened, then remove from the heat and transfer to a shallow bowl.

3 Drain the potato, add to the bowl and crush roughly. Add the chilli flakes, then grate in about half the zest from the lemon. Add salt and pepper and leave to cool.

4 Meanwhile, cut four thin slices off the lemon. Loosen the skin on the breast of each poussin and slide a rosemary sprig and two lemon slices between the meat and the skin.

5 Spoon the mash into the poussin cavities, then rub the butter over the breasts. Season with salt and pepper and place side by side in a shallow roasting tin. Roast for 50 minutes to 1 hour until crisp, golden and cooked through. Serve whole, with simple vegetables.

I do like little poussins – especially for a smart supper for two. They take very well to robust seasonings, such as lemon and rosemary, with a little chilli kick.

Hot lamb baguette with mint and lime

Serves 2

4 thin boneless lamb leg steaks
1 tsp olive oil
2 x 20cm (8 inch) lengths of baguette
2 tsp redcurrant jelly

1 garlic clove, halved
20g (¾oz) mint
1 lime, cut into wedges
sea salt and pepper

1 Preheat a ridged griddle pan. Brush the lamb with the olive oil and cook in the hot pan for about 2 minutes on each side.
2 Meanwhile, split the lengths of baguette and spread the redcurrant jelly on the bases.
3 Transfer the lamb steaks to a large plate and rub with the cut surface of the garlic. Season the lamb with salt and pepper to taste, then place two steaks inside each baguette. Roughly tear in the mint leaves, squeeze in a good measure of lime juice and serve warm.

I love a hot sandwich and, although steak with fried onions and melting cheese is pretty hard to beat, this minty lamb version has an altogether fresher, more vibrant flavour.

Greek-style baked lamb with potatoes

Serves 2

2 tbsp olive oil

1 onion, peeled and sliced

2 garlic cloves, peeled and chopped

2 bone-in lamb leg or shoulder
    steaks

225g (8oz) waxy potatoes, peeled
    and diced

200g (7oz) canned cherry tomatoes

200ml (7fl oz) lamb stock

1 bay leaf

½ tsp dried oregano

6 pitted black olives

sea salt and pepper

1 Preheat the oven to 190°C (fan oven 170°C), gas mark 5. Heat the olive oil
in a small roasting tin and fry the onion and garlic for 3–4 minutes; remove
and set aside.

2 Add the lamb steaks to the roasting tin and brown over a high heat for
2–3 minutes on each side. Return the onion and garlic, add the diced
potatoes and cook for 3 minutes.

3 Add the cherry tomatoes, lamb stock, bay leaf, oregano, black olives and
seasoning. Bake in the oven for 30–40 minutes until the lamb and potatoes
are tender.

An easy braised lamb dish with Mediterranean
flavours. Serve with a simple leafy salad.

Thai beef salad

Illustrated on previous pages

Serves 2

250g (9oz) beef fillet
1 tsp vegetable oil
juice of 1 lime
2 tbsp Thai fish sauce
1 tsp caster sugar
1 shallot, peeled and very thinly sliced

1 garlic clove, peeled and finely chopped
2 tbsp roughly chopped mint or coriander
1 Thai bird's eye chilli, thinly sliced
1 heart of Cos or Romaine lettuce, roughly torn
large handful of bean sprouts

1 Heat a small non-stick frying pan. Rub the beef with the oil and place in the hot pan. Cook over a very high heat for 5 minutes, turning, until well browned all over. Transfer to a plate and leave to rest for 5 minutes.

2 For the dressing, mix the lime juice, fish sauce and caster sugar together in a bowl, then stir in the shallot, garlic, mint and chilli.

3 Pile the torn lettuce on to two serving plates, then scatter over the bean sprouts. Thinly slice the beef and arrange on top. Spoon over the dressing and serve.

This classic Thai salad is very easy to make at home. The beef is only seared on the outside and should be served very rare, so don't be tempted to overcook it. Serve with steamed rice for a delicious and rather elegant supper.

Stir-fried pork and ginger noodles

Serves 2

1 tbsp sunflower oil

200g (7oz) pork stir-fry strips

4cm (1½ inch) piece fresh root
ginger, peeled and shredded

4 spring onions, trimmed and
shredded

1 red chilli, deseeded and thinly
sliced

3 x 150g packets vacuum-packed
udon noodles

2 tbsp soy sauce

juice of 1 small orange

1 tsp oriental chilli oil

1 tsp wine vinegar

handful of basil leaves

1 Heat a wok, then add the oil. When hot, add the pork strips and stir-fry for
5 minutes. Add the ginger, spring onions, chilli and noodles and cook for a
further 2 minutes.

2 Mix the soy sauce, orange juice, chilli oil and vinegar together in a bowl,
then pour into the pan. Toss together well and cook for a further 1 minute
or so until piping hot.

3 Add the basil leaves, toss to mix, then divide the stir-fry between warm
bowls and serve.

A zingy little stir-fry that's cooked and on the
table in under 10 minutes.

Boston baked pork and beans

Serves 4

1 tbsp olive oil
700g (1½lb) belly pork, diced
1 large onion, peeled and diced
2 garlic cloves, peeled and chopped
600ml (1 pint) dry cider
150ml (¼ pint) passata

2 tbsp sun-dried tomato paste
1 tbsp black treacle
1 tbsp brown sugar
1 tsp black mustard seeds
400g can black-eyed beans, drained
sea salt and pepper

1 Preheat the oven to 170°C (fan oven 150°C), gas mark 3. Heat the olive oil in a flameproof casserole and fry the diced belly pork for 5 minutes. Remove with a slotted spoon and set aside.

2 Add the onion and garlic to the casserole and fry gently for about 5 minutes until softened.

3 Stir in the cider, passata, sun-dried tomato paste, black treacle, brown sugar and mustard seeds. Return the pork to the casserole and add the black-eyed beans. Season with salt and pepper, then cover and cook in the oven for 1–1½ hours. Serve with warm crusty bread and a leafy salad.

This wonderful rich casserole freezes well, so eat half now and freeze the rest for another meal for two. Simply thaw overnight in the fridge and reheat thoroughly to serve.

Sausage and lentil casserole

Serves 2

1 tsp olive oil

6 pork sausages

1 small onion, peeled and roughly chopped

2 garlic cloves, peeled and roughly chopped

150g (5oz) Puy lentils

600ml (1 pint) hot chicken stock

1 large tomato, roughly chopped

1 tsp balsamic vinegar

3 tbsp chopped flat leaf parsley

sea salt and pepper

1 Heat the olive oil in a sauté pan and cook the sausages, turning from time to time, for 5–8 minutes until golden on all sides. Add the onion and garlic and cook for 2–3 minutes until beginning to soften.

2 Add the lentils, stock and chopped tomato. Bring to the boil, then cover and simmer very gently for 40–45 minutes until the lentils are tender and most of the stock has been absorbed.

3 Stir in the balsamic vinegar and parsley and add salt and pepper to taste. Spoon into warm bowls and serve with crusty bread.

I always keep a variety of dried lentils in stock as they're fantastic for stews and soups. The Puy lentil has a lovely texture and flavour but if you're serving this dish for supper, you can use everyday brown or green lentils.

Ricotta and basil frittata

Serves 2

2 tbsp olive oil
5 eggs
2 slices of white bread, crusts
   removed
1 garlic clove, peeled and crushed
20g (¾oz) basil, finely chopped
150g (5oz) ricotta cheese
sea salt and pepper

1 Preheat the grill to high. Heat a splash of the olive oil in a 20cm (8 inch) frying pan. Beat the eggs in a large bowl, then tear in the white bread and season with salt and pepper. Pour into the pan and cook very gently for 5 minutes.

2 Meanwhile, in a pestle and mortar, pound together the garlic and basil to make a paste. Stir in the remaining olive oil and season with salt and pepper.

3 Drop spoonfuls of the ricotta on to the fritatta, then drizzle over the basil dressing. Cook for a further 2–3 minutes until the frittata is almost totally set, then finish cooking under the hot grill for 3–4 minutes until completely set and golden brown.

4 Slide the frittata out of the pan on to a board and cut into wedges. Serve with a tomato and onion salad, and good crusty bread.

Here I've used the traditional southern Italian method of tearing some fresh white bread into the beaten eggs to give the frittata a firm, almost cake-like texture.

Butter bean and mozzarella burgers

Serves 2

4 spring onions, trimmed and thickly sliced

1 garlic clove, peeled and thickly sliced

410g can butter beans, drained

100g (3½oz) fresh white breadcrumbs

1 egg yolk

150g (5oz) mozzarella cheese, drained and diced

pinch of cayenne pepper

2–3 tbsp vegetable oil

sea salt and pepper

To serve

2 crusty rolls, split open

1 ripe tomato, sliced

mayonnaise

1 Put the spring onions and garlic into a food processor and whiz until finely chopped. Add the beans and whiz again to form a coarse purée. Add the breadcrumbs, egg yolk, mozzarella, cayenne and some salt and pepper. Pulse to form a stiff paste.

2 Shape the mixture into two even-sized burgers. Heat the oil in a heavy-based non-stick frying pan. Shallow-fry the burgers for 3–4 minutes on each side until golden – the cheese may ooze out and make the burgers stick a little, so make sure you use a good non-stick pan.

3 Drain the burgers on kitchen paper. Serve in the crusty rolls with a few slices of tomato and a good dollop of mayonnaise.

These juicy, succulent burgers have delicious pockets of molten mozzarella inside. Butter beans lend a lovely creamy texture and go well with aromatics like spring onions and garlic.

family feasts

Roast salmon and goat's cheese salad

Serves 12

1 baguette, cut into 1cm (½ inch) slices

3–4 tbsp olive oil

6 pieces of salmon fillet, each about 250g (9oz)

2 Romaine lettuces, sliced or torn into large pieces

1 large cucumber, peeled and thinly sliced

20g (¾oz) mint, roughly torn

20g (¾oz) chives, snipped

200g (7oz) cooked beetroot, thinly sliced

400g (14oz) medium soft goat's cheese

For the dressing

3 tbsp olive oil

1 tbsp red wine vinegar

pinch of caster sugar

sea salt and pepper

1 Preheat the oven to 220°C (fan oven 200°C), gas mark 7. Arrange the slices of bread on baking sheets and brush lightly with olive oil, then sprinkle with a little sea salt. Bake for 10–12 minutes until golden brown. Leave to cool on a wire rack, then pile these crostini on a serving board.

2 Arrange the salmon fillets on a baking sheet. Brush with a little olive oil and season with salt and pepper. Bake for 12–15 minutes until golden and just cooked. Leave to cool.

3 Scatter the lettuce on a large serving platter. Add the cucumber, mint, chives and beetroot. Crumble over the goat's cheese. Flake the salmon and scatter on top.

4 Mix together the dressing ingredients and drizzle over the salad. Serve fairly swiftly, with the crostini on the side.

With its mix of pinks and greens, this salad looks gorgeous casually presented on a large platter. Prepare all the elements, such as the crostini and salmon, ahead of time and just assemble when ready to serve.

Smoked salmon tart

Illustrated on previous pages

Serves 6

225g (8oz) plain flour
½ tsp salt
125g (4oz) chilled butter, diced
1 tsp dried chilli flakes
450ml (¾ pint) double cream
2 large eggs

2 egg yolks
100g (3½oz) Parmesan cheese,
  freshly grated
200g (7oz) smoked salmon, roughly
  torn into strips
sea salt and pepper

1 Preheat the oven to 200°C (fan oven 180°C), gas mark 6. Place the flour, salt, butter and chilli flakes in a food processor and whiz until the mixtures forms fine crumbs. Pour in 3 tbsp very cold water and pulse again briefly, to form a firm dough.

2 Roll out the pastry on a lightly floured surface and use to line a 22cm (8½ inch) loose-bottomed flan tin. Use a rolling pin to lift the pastry into the tin. Press the pastry well into the sides, then trim away excess pastry overhanging the tin.

3 Prick the bottom of the pastry case with a fork, then fill with crumpled foil and bake for 10 minutes. Take the pastry case out of the oven and remove the foil. Lower the oven temperature to 180°C (fan oven 160°C), gas mark 4.

4 Beat together the cream, whole eggs and egg yolks until well blended. Stir in the Parmesan and smoked salmon and season with some salt and pepper. Pour into the pastry case. Bake for 25 minutes until the filling is just set.

5 Carefully remove the tart from the tin and cut into slices to serve while it is still warm.

This is perfect for a family feast. Make two tarts in the morning and keep in a cool, dry place – not the fridge or the pastry will go soggy. Serve with a simple salad for an elegant lunch.

Oriental roast chicken

Illustrated on previous pages

Serves 12

3 large chickens, each about 2kg
  (4½lb), quartered
4 garlic cloves, peeled and roughly
  chopped
4 shallots, peeled and roughly
  chopped
4cm (1½ inch) piece fresh root ginger,
  peeled and roughly chopped

4 lemon grass stalks, roughly
  chopped
3 tbsp light muscovado sugar
2 tbsp Thai fish sauce
300ml (½ pint) chicken stock
juice of 1 lime
sea salt and pepper
6 spring onions, trimmed and thinly
  sliced, to serve

1 Deeply slash each chicken quarter 2 or 3 times and nestle them into a very large roasting tin (or use two regular tins).

2 Pound the garlic, shallots, ginger, lemon grass and 2 tbsp of the sugar together, using a pestle and mortar to make a coarse paste. Stir in the fish sauce. Rub the mixture over the chicken pieces, making sure it goes into the slashes. Leave in a cool place for at least 2 hours (ideally overnight in the fridge), turning from time to time.

3 Preheat the oven to 200°C (fan oven 180°C), gas mark 6. Sprinkle the chicken quarters with some coarse sea salt and roast for 45–50 minutes until beautifully crisp and brown, and cooked through. To check, insert a skewer into the thickest part of the thigh; the juices should run clear and not at all pink. When the chicken is cooked, transfer to a warmed large serving platter and set aside in a warm spot to rest for 5 minutes.

4 Pour away any fat from the roasting tin, then place the tin on the hob and pour in the stock. Bring to the boil, stirring to loosen any residue from the bottom of the tin. Simmer for a couple of minutes, then add the lime juice and the remaining sugar, to taste.

5 Pour the sauce over the chicken, scatter with spring onions and serve with rice and steamed Chinese greens.

Moroccan chicken and pastina bake

Illustrated on previous pages

Serves 10

500g (1lb 2oz) cherry tomatoes
10 chicken thighs
1 garlic bulb, broken into cloves
1 tbsp olive oil
1 large red onion, peeled and thinly
    sliced
700g (1½lb) dried conchigliette, or
    other tiny dried pasta shapes

2 cinnamon sticks, broken in half
1 tsp cumin seeds
2 litres (3½ pints) hot chicken stock
grated zest and juice of 1 large
    orange
20g (¾oz) flat leaf parsley, roughly
    chopped
sea salt and pepper

1 Preheat the oven to 200°C (fan oven 180°C), gas mark 6. Put the cherry
tomatoes into a very large roasting tin and nestle the chicken thighs and
garlic cloves among them (or use two regular tins). Drizzle over the olive oil
and season with salt and pepper. Bake for 15 minutes.

2 Scatter the red onion slices over the chicken pieces and bake for a further
5 minutes.

3 Now stir in the pasta, cinnamon, cumin, stock, orange zest and juice,
and a little more seasoning. Return to the oven and bake for a further
15–20 minutes or until the pasta is cooked and the liquid has been absorbed.
Stir through the chopped parsley and serve straight from the tin.

This is a big, hearty family bake with a North
African flavour. As it cooks the top of the
pasta becomes golden and a little crunchy.

Minted chicken and new potato salad

Serves 12

2 roast chickens, each about 1.5kg (3¼lb)

1.5kg (3¼lb) baby new potatoes, halved if large

250g (9oz) fine green beans, trimmed

4 tbsp pine nuts, toasted

1 bunch of spring onions, trimmed and sliced

For the minty dressing

3 tbsp Greek yogurt

3 tbsp olive oil

pinch of sugar

20g (¾oz) mint

sea salt and pepper

1 Remove the legs and breasts from the roast chickens. Tear the breast meat into bite-sized pieces and place in a large wide serving bowl. Remove the leg meat from the bones and tear it into similar pieces; add to the bowl. Strip any meat from the chicken carcasses and add this too. Set aside.

2 Cook the potatoes in boiling salted water for 10–12 minutes until tender. Add the beans for the last 2–3 minutes of cooking. Drain well and cool under cold running water. Drain and pat dry on kitchen paper. Add to the chicken together with the pine nuts and spring onions and mix well.

3 To make the dressing, whisk together the yogurt, olive oil, 3 tbsp water, sugar and some salt and pepper. Set aside a few mint leaves to garnish; finely chop the rest and stir into the dressing.

4 Pour the dressing over the salad, tossing to make sure everything is coated. Scatter with the reserved mint leaves and serve.

This summer salad is ideal for outdoor eating. Either buy ready-roasted chickens from your butcher or supermarket or, better still, roast your own. Allow 1½ hours at 200°C (fan oven 180°C), gas mark 6 for 1.5kg (3½lb) chickens.

Roast lamb with sticky pancetta potatoes

Serves 6–8

1 whole shoulder of lamb, about
   2.5kg (5½lb)
2 garlic cloves, peeled and finely
   chopped
20g (¾oz) mint, finely chopped
1 tsp dried oregano

3 tbsp olive oil
1.5–2kg (3¼–4½lb) red-skinned
   potatoes, such as Desirée, scrubbed
125g (4oz) cubed pancetta
2 red onions, thinly sliced
100ml (3½fl oz) dry cider
sea salt and pepper

1 First weigh the lamb to estimate the cooking time – it needs 30 minutes per kilo (2¼lb) plus 20 minutes, so for a 2.5kg (5½lb) joint, you will need to cook it for 1 hour and 35 minutes.

2 Place the lamb on a rack set over a roasting tin. Using a skewer, deeply pierce the meat in several places. Stir together the garlic, mint, oregano, olive oil and some salt and pepper. Brush all over the lamb, then set aside for at least an hour.

3 Preheat the oven to 200°C (fan oven 180°C), gas mark 6. Cook the whole potatoes in a pan of boiling salted water for 15 minutes. Drain, then cut into 2cm (¾ inch) thick slices.

4 Lift the lamb on its rack off the roasting tin and scatter the sliced potatoes, pancetta and onions into the tin. Season with salt and pepper and pour over the cider. Replace the rack and roast the lamb according to your estimation.

5 Transfer the lamb to a warm platter and leave to rest in a warm spot for 15 minutes before carving. Turn the oven off and put the tin of potatoes back in to keep warm while the meat is resting. Serve the lamb with the sticky pancetta potatoes.

You will need to ask the butcher to leave the shoulder whole for this dish. For large feasts, quantities can easily be doubled.

Crusty-topped shepherd's pie

Serves 12

3 tbsp olive oil

3 onions, peeled and chopped

4 garlic cloves, peeled and chopped

4 carrots, peeled and diced

2 tsp caraway seeds

1.5kg (3¼lb) lean lamb mince

1 small Savoy cabbage, sliced

1.5 litres (2½ pints) chicken stock

6 tbsp brown sauce

300g (11oz) frozen peas

20g (¾oz) flat leaf parsley, roughly
chopped

For the Cheddar mash

2kg (4½lb) floury potatoes such as
Maris Piper or King Edward,
peeled and cubed

150ml (¼ pint) milk

50g (2oz) butter

250g (9oz) mature Cheddar cheese,
grated

sea salt and pepper

1 Heat the olive oil in a large roasting tin set on the hob. Add the onions, garlic, carrots and caraway seeds and cook for 3–4 minutes. Add the mince and cook for a further 5–10 minutes, stirring now and again, until browned.
2 Drain off any excess fat, then stir in the cabbage and cook for another couple of minutes. Add the stock and brown sauce. Bring to the boil, then simmer very gently for 30 minutes.
3 Meanwhile, make the mash. Cook the potatoes in boiling salted water for 15–20 minutes until tender. Drain well, then mash and stir in the milk, butter, cheese and seasoning.
4 Preheat the oven to 180°C (fan oven 160°C), gas mark 4. Stir the peas and parsley into the mince and season with salt and pepper. Spread out smoothly, then spoon over the mash and rough up the surface with the back of a spoon. Bake for 45 minutes until bubbling and golden.

This is an absolute winner on any family table. My version is flavoured with caraway seeds and topped with a tasty Cheddar mash.

Boiled beef and carrots with herb dumplings

Serves 10

40g (1½oz) lard, or 2 tbsp
 vegetable oil
2kg (4½lb) chuck steak, cut into
 large cubes
4 tbsp plain flour
4 onions, peeled and sliced
1.5kg (3¼lb) carrots, peeled and
 thickly sliced
2 bay leaves
3 rosemary sprigs

500ml (16fl oz) red wine
1.5 litres (2½ pints) hot beef stock
sea salt and pepper

For the dumplings
250g (9oz) self-raising flour
1 tsp baking powder
½ tsp table salt
125g (4oz) suet
20g (¾oz) flat leaf parsley or chives,
 finely chopped

1 Preheat the oven to 170°C (fan oven 150°C), gas mark 3. Set the roasting tin on the hob and add the lard to melt.
2 Meanwhile, toss the meat in the flour to coat lightly. Add to the tin and cook for 10 minutes, stirring fairly frequently, until nicely browned. Remove and set aside.
3 Add the onions to the roasting tin and brown them, then add the carrots, bay leaves, rosemary, wine and stock. Return the browned beef and add some seasoning. Bring to the boil. Cover with foil and transfer to the oven to cook for 2 hours until the meat is tender.
4 To make the dumplings, place the flour in a large bowl and stir in the baking powder, salt, suet and herbs. Stir in enough water – about 150ml (¼ pint) – to make a soft dough. Don't worry if it's a little sticky. Roll into 20 balls, each about the size of a cherry.
5 Drop the dumplings into the stew and continue cooking, still covered for 30–35 minutes until the dumplings are puffed and cooked through.

This is a proper old-fashioned, warming stew. If you have a very large casserole, do use it otherwise a sturdy, deep roasting tin is fine.

Succulent pork roast

Illustrated on previous pages

Serves 10–12

1 boneless shoulder of pork, about
  4kg (9lb)
20g (¾oz) rosemary sprigs
50g (2oz) Parmesan cheese, freshly
  grated

4 garlic cloves, peeled and finely
  chopped
40g (1½oz) flat leaf parsley, chopped
sea salt and pepper

1 If you want the pork to have a soft, chewy skin, which is traditional for this dish, then preheat the oven now to 190°C (fan oven 170°C), gas mark 5.

2 Remove the leaves from 2 sprigs of rosemary and roughly chop. Cut the strings on the pork and open it out on a flat surface. Season generously with salt and pepper, then evenly sprinkle over the Parmesan, garlic and chopped rosemary and parsley.

3 Roll up the pork again to enclose the filling. Tie with string at 2cm (¾ inch) intervals to keep the meat in shape. If the skin is not already scored, use a small very sharp knife to score it between the strings. Sprinkle with salt, then slip the remaining rosemary sprigs under the strings.

4 For a soft, chewy skin, roast the pork straightaway, allowing 20 minutes per 500g (1lb 2oz) plus 20 minutes – if your joint weighs 4kg (9lb), it will take 3 hours. If you want the pork to have a crunchy crackling (which will make it harder to carve), leave it for at least 2 hours before cooking. Then, before putting it in to roast, pat with kitchen paper to dry off the excess water. Roast at the same temperature, turning up the oven to 220°C (fan oven 200°C), gas mark 7 for the last 20 minutes of the cooking time.

5 Leave the pork to rest for a good 30 minutes before carving. Serve warm.

This is based on a classic Italian dish known as porchetta. I find that shoulder of pork is the best cut to use as it has exactly the right balance of meat and fat.

Roasted carrots with garlic and parsley

Serves 4–6
500g (1lb 2oz) carrots, scrubbed
1–2 tbsp olive oil
caster sugar, to sprinkle
handful of garlic cloves, unpeeled
splash of balsamic vinegar, to drizzle
sea salt
handful of chopped flat leaf parsley,
    to serve

1 Preheat the oven to 190°C (fan oven 170°C), gas mark 5. Cut the carrots into 1 cm (½ inch) thick slices and place in a roasting tin. Drizzle with a little olive oil and sprinkle lightly with sugar and salt. Toss to mix and roast in the oven for 15 minutes.
2 Scatter over the unpeeled garlic cloves and roast for a further 30 minutes until the carrots and garlic are tender and golden brown.
3 Drizzle with balsamic vinegar and scatter over chopped parsley to serve.

This effortless, flavourful accompaniment can easily be doubled or tripled to serve a larger gathering.

Sesame, green bean and radish salad

Serves 4–6

450g (1lb) fine green beans, trimmed

5 radishes, trimmed and thinly
  sliced

sea salt

toasted sesame seeds, to serve

For the dressing

3 tbsp sunflower oil

1 garlic clove, peeled and thinly
  sliced

2 tsp toasted sesame oil

1 tbsp light soy sauce

1 Add the green beans to a pan of boiling salted water and blanch for
2–3 minutes, then drain and refresh under cold running water.

2 For the dressing, heat the sunflower oil in a small frying pan and sauté
the sliced garlic until just turning golden, then transfer to a bowl. Whisk in
the toasted sesame oil and light soy sauce.

3 Combine the beans and radishes in a serving dish and pour over the
dressing. Scatter with some toasted sesame seeds and serve.

This oriental-style salad can be prepared well
ahead – convenient if you are entertaining.

Clapshot

Serves 4–6

500g (1lb 2oz) swede
500g (1lb 2oz) floury potatoes, such
   as Maris Piper or King Edward
2 rashers of dry-cured streaky
   bacon, snipped into pieces
4 spring onions, trimmed and thinly
   sliced
splash of warm milk
sea salt and pepper

1 Peel the swede and potatoes, cut into chunks and add to a pan of lightly
salted water. Bring to the boil and simmer until tender.
2 Meanwhile, cook the bacon in a dry frying pan until crisp and golden,
then add the sliced spring onions and cook for 1 minute.
3 Drain the swede and potatoes and mash well. Beat in the bacon and spring
onions, together with a splash of warm milk. Season with salt and pepper to
taste and serve.

This flavoured mash of 'tatties and neeps' goes
brilliantly with warming stews. It can easily
be made in larger quantities to feed a crowd.

Long stem broccoli with chilli and lemon

Serves 4–6

1 head of broccoli
2 tbsp sunflower oil
1–2 garlic cloves, peeled and thinly
  sliced
1–2 red chillies, sliced
juice of ½ lemon
sea salt and pepper

1 Trim the base of the stalk from the head of broccoli, then cut into long florets, leaving a good length of stalk on each. Cook the broccoli in a pan of boiling salted water for 2 minutes, then drain thoroughly.
2 Heat the sunflower oil in a non-stick frying pan and cook the sliced garlic for a few seconds. Add the broccoli and sliced red chillies, and stir-fry for 2–3 minutes until the broccoli is tender but still firm.
3 Add the lemon juice and salt and pepper to taste. Serve at once.

This is an interesting way to liven up broccoli. To accompany the main courses in this chapter simply increase the quantities accordingly.

family puddings

Lemonade granita

Serves 6
175g (6oz) caster sugar
grated zest and juice of 6 lemons
1 lemon grass stalk, roughly
   flattened with a rolling pin
450ml (¾ pint) soda water

1 Put the sugar, lemon zest and juice, and lemon grass stalk into a saucepan
with 150ml (¼ pint) water. Heat gently, stirring, until the sugar dissolves,
then simmer gently for 5 minutes. Leave to cool.
2 Strain the liquid into a rigid container and stir in the soda water. Freeze
for 2 hours until almost firm, then use a fork to break the mixture into
large flaky crystals. Freeze for a further 2 hours, then break up again.
Spoon into small tumblers for serving.

This beautifully textured granita will keep in
the freezer for weeks, but may then need a
firm hand to break up the crystals.

Frozen berry yogurt and meringue pots

Makes 6

250g (9oz) frozen summer berries
75g (3oz) icing sugar
4 tbsp blackcurrant cordial
500g (1lb 2oz) Greek yogurt
2 meringue nests, crumbled

1 Put the frozen fruit into a bowl, sift the icing sugar over, then drizzle with the blackcurrant cordial. Roughly break up the fruit with a fork.
2 Tip the yogurt into a bowl and beat with a wooden spoon to soften. Ripple through the fruit mixture with the crumbled meringues.
3 Spoon into six small freezerproof glasses and freeze for 2–3 hours until firm. If you freeze for longer than this, take the pots out of the freezer 10–20 minutes before serving, to soften up.

This simple berry fruit ice with nuggets of melt-in-the-mouth meringue is incredibly easy to prepare.

Bellini jellies

Illustrated on previous pages

Serves 6

600ml (1 pint) dry white wine
175g (6oz) caster sugar
5 sheets of leaf gelatine
1 large peach
4 tbsp peach schnapps
1 pink rose

1 Place the wine and sugar in a small pan and simmer gently, stirring, until the sugar dissolves.

2 Meanwhile, soak the gelatine leaves in a shallow dish of cold water until softened, then drain and squeeze out the excess water. Remove the wine from the heat, add the gelatine leaves and stir until melted. Set aside to cool.

3 Cut a cross in the skin at the base of the peach, then plunge into boiling water. Leave for 1 minute, then remove. Using a small knife, peel off all the skin. Halve, remove the stone and roughly chop the flesh. Purée in a mini chopper until smooth, then pass through a sieve.

4 Once the wine is at room temperature, stir in the peach purée and schnapps, then pour into six moulds or ramekins. Carefully pull some of the petals from the rose and float a couple of rose petals on each jelly. Chill for at least 3 hours until set.

5 To serve, dip the moulds briefly into hot water, then turn out the jellies on to small plates. Decorate with more rose petals (and the rosebud if you like).

Here the classic Venetian cocktail is made into a gently wobbling dessert. Make ahead and serve as the ultimate dinner party finale, or between courses as a palate cleanser.

Chocolate banana cups

Serves 6
200g (7oz) luxury dark chocolate,
    in pieces
500g carton fresh custard
2 bananas, chopped

1 Melt the chocolate in a heatproof bowl set over a pan of simmering water
or in the microwave.
2 Pour the custard into a large bowl and, using an electric mixer, gradually
whisk in the melted chocolate until the mixture is smooth and well blended.
3 Stir in the chopped bananas, then pour into six cups or glasses and place
in the fridge to chill and set.

When you haven't time to make a real pudding
and you want something more than fresh
fruit, try this simple dessert.

Little apricot and lavender mousses

Serves 6

1kg (2¼lb) apricots, stoned and
  roughly chopped
½ tsp lavender flowers or 2 rosemary
  sprigs
125g (4oz) caster sugar
1 sheet of leaf gelatine
1 egg white
150ml (¼ pint) double cream

1 Combine the apricots, lavender, caster sugar and 5 tbsp water in a saucepan. Cook gently for 15–20 minutes, stirring from time to time, until the fruit is pulpy and almost smooth.

2 Soak the leaf gelatine in a shallow dish of cold water until softened, then drain and squeeze out the excess water. Remove the apricot mixture from the heat and stir in the leaf gelatine, until melted. Leave to cool. (If you used rosemary in place of the lavender, remove the sprig at this stage.)

3 Whisk the egg white until it forms firm peaks. Whip the cream in another bowl until thick. Fold the egg white and cream into the cooled apricot mixture. Spoon into individual pots or glasses and chill for at least 2 hours until nicely set.

Make these light-as-air fruit mousses in early summer when fragrant apricots are in season.

Raspberry slush

Serves 4

250g (9oz) frozen raspberries
4 tbsp lime cordial
200–250ml (7–8fl oz) lemonade

1 Put the frozen raspberries into a food processor with the lime cordial and lemonade and whiz to make a coarse slush.
2 Pour into glasses and serve immediately.

This speedy dessert is wonderfully refreshing and takes only minutes to prepare.

Stir-fried toffee pineapple

Serves 3–4
432g can pineapple chunks in
    natural juice, drained
large knob of butter
2 tbsp light soft brown sugar
2 tbsp desiccated coconut

1 Pat the canned pineapple chunks dry on kitchen paper. Heat the butter in
a frying pan and add the pineapple, brown sugar and desiccated coconut.
Cook, stirring, over a high heat for 4–5 minutes until the pineapple chunks
are golden brown.
2 Serve straightaway, with scoops of vanilla ice cream.

This is a convenient dessert made entirely
from storecupboard ingredients. If you happen
to have a fresh pineapple in the fruit bowl,
then feel free to use it!

Panettone bruschetta with berry compote

Serves 4

150ml (¼ pint) freshly squeezed
   orange juice
1 vanilla pod, halved lengthways
1 star anise
50g (2oz) caster sugar
300g (11oz) mixed summer fruits,
   such as raspberries, strawberries
   and blueberries

4 large slices of panettone
50g (2oz) butter, melted
2 tbsp icing sugar
4 tbsp Greek yogurt or extra
   thick cream

1 Heat the orange juice in a small pan with the split vanilla pod, star anise and caster sugar. Bring to a gentle boil, then remove from the heat. Stir in the fruit and leave to cool completely, then chill until ready to serve.
2 Preheat a griddle pan. Brush the panettone with the melted butter, then dust with icing sugar. Toast on the griddle pan for 1–2 minutes on each side until crisp and golden brown.
3 Divide the griddled panettone among four plates and spoon over the fruit compote, discarding the vanilla pod and star anise. Top each portion with a spoonful of yogurt and serve.

This spectacular summer dessert of sugar-toasted slices of panettone topped with juicy soft fruits can double as a brilliant breakfast.

Blueberry pancakes

Serves 4

150g (5oz) plain flour
2 tbsp caster sugar, plus extra
   to sprinkle
pinch of salt
2 eggs
5 tbsp milk
125g (4oz) blueberries
a little sunflower oil, for cooking

1 Mix the flour, caster sugar and salt together in a large bowl and make a well in the centre.
2 Whisk the eggs and milk together, then pour into the well. Gradually mix into the flour, then beat with a whisk until you have a smooth batter. Stir in the blueberries.
3 Cook the pancakes in batches. Heat just a tiny splash of sunflower oil in a non-stick frying pan. Add spoonfuls of the mixture, spacing them well apart and cook for 1–2 minutes on each side until puffed and golden. Remove and stack on a warm plate; keep warm while you cook the rest.
4 Serve the pancakes warm, sprinkled with a little sugar.

These irresistible fruity pancakes are delicious served with a drizzle of pouring cream. They are also great for a leisurely breakfast.

Strawberry clafoutis

Illustrated on previous pages

Serves 4

4 eggs
150g (5oz) caster sugar
150ml (¼ pint) double cream
1 tbsp plain flour
1 tbsp ground almonds
grated zest of 1 lime
225g (8oz) strawberries, halved
   if large

1 Preheat the oven to 190°C (fan oven 170°C), gas mark 5. Using an electric mixer, beat the eggs with the sugar until really thick and voluminous.
2 Lightly whip the cream until it forms soft peaks. Fold the cream into the egg mixture together with the flour, ground almonds and lime zest.
3 Divide the strawberries among four heatproof bowls or individual gratin dishes. Spoon over the batter and bake for 12 minutes until golden. Serve warm, topped with a scoop of vanilla ice cream.

Although this is an incredibly simple dessert, it looks very stylish, which makes it perfect for entertaining. I love to eat warm clafoutis topped with a scoop of melting ice cream.

Soggy belly chocolate fudge cake

Illustrated on previous pages

Serves 8

200g (7oz) luxury dark chocolate, in
 pieces
140g (4½oz) butter
3 tbsp Irish cream liqueur or
 whiskey

5 eggs, separated
200g (7oz) vanilla caster sugar or
 regular caster sugar
100g (3½oz) plain flour
1 tsp baking powder

1 Preheat the oven to 180°C (fan oven 160°C), gas mark 4. Line a 23cm
(9 inch) springform cake tin with silicone paper or baking parchment.
2 Put the chocolate, butter and liqueur into a large heatproof bowl set over a
pan of gently simmering water and heat until melted. Remove from the heat
and allow to cool for a couple of minutes. Stir until smooth.
3 Meanwhile, whisk the egg whites in a clean bowl until they form soft
peaks. Gradually whisk in the sugar, a tablespoonful at a time.
4 Stir the eggs yolks into the chocolate mixture, then fold in the whisked
egg white mixture. Sift over the flour and baking powder, and gently fold in
using a large metal spoon.
5 Pour the mixture into the prepared tin and bake for 30–40 minutes until
just set. Leave to cool in the tin for at least 20 minutes, then gently lift out
of the tin and cut into wedges to serve.

Here is a scrummy cross between a classic chocolate cake and a fudgy-centred brownie. It is best eaten on the day it is made, while still warm, which shouldn't be too much trouble. Serve with pouring cream or vanilla ice cream.

Best ever vanilla cheesecake

Serves 10
200g (7oz) gingernut biscuits
50g (2oz) butter, melted
1 vanilla pod
3 x 250g tubs mascarpone cheese
125g (4oz) caster sugar
2 tbsp cornflour
3 eggs
grated zest of 1 lemon

1 Preheat the oven to 180°C (fan oven 160°C), gas mark 4. Put the biscuits into a strong polythene bag and crush with a rolling pin. Tip into a large bowl. Stir in the melted butter until evenly mixed.
2 Turn the crumb mixture into a 23cm (9 inch) non-stick springform cake tin, pressing the crumbs down firmly with the back of a spoon. Place in the fridge to chill for 5–10 minutes.
3 Using a small knife, slit open the vanilla pod and scrape the seeds into a large bowl. Add the mascarpone, sugar, cornflour, eggs and lemon zest, and beat with an electric mixer until smooth.
4 Pour the mixture into the cake tin and place on a baking sheet. Bake for 45 minutes or until golden – the filling will still be a little wobbly at this stage. Turn off the oven, open the door and leave the cheesecake inside until completely cool – the filling will set as it cools. Cut into wedges to serve.

Most cheesecakes are good but, with its fantastic texture and light lemon and vanilla flavour, this one is unbeatable. Keep it in the fridge and cut slices off it all week.

Coffee cream trifle

Serves 8

150g (5oz) cantuccini biscuits
100ml (3½fl oz) strong black coffee
4 tbsp Marsala or dessert wine
300ml (½ pint) double cream
500g (1lb 2oz) Greek yogurt
6 tbsp demerara sugar

1 Break the biscuits roughly into a glass serving bowl and pour over the coffee and Marsala. Leave to soak for 10 minutes or so.
2 Meanwhile, whip the cream until it forms soft peaks, then stir in the yogurt. Spoon over the biscuits and sprinkle the sugar on top. Cover and chill overnight.

This simple trifle needs a night in the fridge so it's a perfect prepare-ahead dessert. The sugar melts into the cream overnight, leaving a scrumptious syrupy layer on the surface.

Melting chocolate risotto

Serves 6

750ml (1¼ pints) milk
50g (2oz) light muscovado sugar
50g (2oz) butter
½ tsp ground cinnamon
125g (4oz) risotto rice, such as
   carnaroli or arborio
100g (3½oz) luxury dark chocolate,
   roughly chopped

1 Put the milk and muscovado sugar into a pan and heat gently until the sugar dissolves.
2 Melt the butter in a large non-stick pan and stir in the cinnamon and rice. Cook for 1 minute, then add half of the hot sugared milk and cook for 10 minutes, stirring from time to time. Pour in the remaining hot milk and stir and cook for a further 8–10 minutes until the rice is tender and the milk has been absorbed.
3 Scatter over the chocolate and stir to ripple through roughly. Spoon into bowls and serve warm. Alternatively, spoon the rice pudding into glasses and chill before serving.

What could be better than rice pudding? Chocolate rice pudding! And this one is an absolute stunner…

Snowy saffron peaches

Illustrated on previous pages

Serves 6

50g (2oz) butter
6 large, ripe peaches, halved
1 tbsp roughly chopped pistachio
   nuts
65g (2½oz) caster sugar
small pinch of saffron threads
1 egg white

1 Preheat the oven to 200°C (fan oven 180°C), gas mark 6. Melt the butter in a small roasting tin in the oven, then put in the peach halves in one layer. Scatter in the nuts. Roast for 25 minutes, turning from time to time, until the peaches are tender and golden.
2 Meanwhile, whiz the caster sugar with the saffron in a mini chopper or blender until well blended. Whisk the egg white in a clean bowl to stiff peaks, then gradually whisk in the saffron sugar to make a firm, glossy meringue.
3 Turn the peach halves hollow side up. Spoon a peak of meringue on top of each one. Return to the oven to bake for 5 minutes until lightly tinged with brown. Serve hot, with the pan juices drizzled round.

Roasting really brings out the natural sweetness of ripe peaches. The snowy saffron meringues finish them off with a stylish flourish. Serve with vanilla ice cream.

Treacle tart

Serves 10

225g (8oz) plain flour, plus extra
   to dust
150g (5oz) cold butter, diced
1 egg yolk
1 tsp golden caster sugar

For the filling

800g (1¾lb) golden syrup
125g (4oz) fresh white breadcrumbs
finely grated zest of 2 lemons
50g (2oz) porridge oats
2 eggs, beaten

1 Preheat the oven to 180°C (fan oven 160°C), gas mark 4. Put the flour and butter into a food processor and pulse until the mixture forms fine crumbs. Add the egg yolk, sugar and 2 tbsp cold water and pulse again briefly until the mixture comes together into a dough.

2 Roll out the dough on a lightly floured surface and use to line a fluted, deep, loose-bottomed 24cm (9½ inch) flan tin. Prick the bottom and chill for 30 minutes.

3 To make the filling, warm the golden syrup in a pan until runny but not too hot. Remove from the heat and stir in the breadcrumbs, lemon zest, oats and beaten eggs.

4 Pour the filling into the pastry case. Bake for 30–40 minutes until the filling is golden and just set; don't worry if it is still a little soft. Leave to cool in the tin for a few minutes, then carefully lift out. Cut the tart into slices to serve.

The sweetness of the syrup and the zesty bite of lemon in this tart never fail to please.

Old-fashioned coconut and jam tart

Serves 8
375g (13oz) ready-made sweet
  shortcrust pastry
flour, to dust
3 eggs

125g (4oz) golden caster sugar
200ml carton coconut cream
75g (3oz) desiccated coconut
75g (3oz) plain flour
4 tbsp seedless raspberry jam

1 Preheat the oven to 200°C (fan oven 180°C), gas mark 6. Roll out the pastry on a lightly floured surface and use to line a fluted, deep, loose-bottomed 24cm (9½ inch) flan tin. If you have time, rest in the fridge for 30 minutes. Prick the pastry lightly with a fork, fill with crumpled foil and bake for 15 minutes until set.

2 Using an electric mixer, beat the eggs and sugar together until thick and voluminous. Gently stir in the coconut cream, desiccated coconut and flour.

3 Reduce the oven temperature to 180°C (fan oven 160°C), gas mark 4. Lift the foil out of the pastry case, then spread the jam over the bottom. Pour in the coconut mixture.

4 Bake for 30–40 minutes until the filling is set and golden. Leave to cool in the tin for a few minutes, then carefully lift out, slice and serve.

A wonderful moist tart, this has a classic 'teatime'-style layer of red jam between the pastry and coconut filling. It beats any shop-bought version hands down.

Oaty ginger pear crumble

Serves 8

8 dessert pears, such as Rocha
50g (2oz) butter
50g (2oz) light muscovado sugar
4 pieces of stem ginger in syrup,
  drained and finely chopped
juice of 1 lemon

For the crumble topping

150g (5oz) cold butter, diced
300g (11oz) plain flour
100g (3½oz) rolled oats
175g (6oz) light muscovado sugar

1 Preheat the oven to 180°C (fan oven 160°C), gas mark 4. Peel, quarter and core the pears, then cut into chunks. Put the butter into a pan with the pears, sugar, ginger and lemon juice and cook gently for 10 minutes.
2 Meanwhile, make the crumble topping. Rub the butter into the flour until there are no large pieces left. Stir in the oats and sugar.
3 Spoon the fruit mixture into a large ovenproof dish and scatter over the crumble mixture. Bake for 40–45 minutes until nicely browned. Serve with hot custard.

Crumble is one of the easiest and most comforting puddings. The stem ginger in this filling gives every mouthful a little zing.

Index

A

almonds: rough raspberry and almond slice, 188

anchovies: quattro stagioni baking tray tart, 230

antipasti, Italian, 114

apricots: banana, apricot and orange blitz, 46

little apricot and lavender mousses, 271

artichoke hearts: Italian antipasti, 114

aubergines: aubergine, feta and broad bean salad, 148

skewered lamb and aubergine pittas, 168

B

bacon: clapshot, 255

English breakfast salad, 33

fusilli with cabbage and crispy bacon, 85

bagels: mozzarella and tomato bagel melt, 32

baked beans: cheesy bean hash, 103

bananas: banana, apricot and orange blitz, 46

chocolate banana cups, 270

cinnamon pancakes, 40–1

bean sprouts: Vietnamese beef noodles, 78–9

beans: Boston baked pork and beans, 211

butter bean and mozzarella burgers, 217

cheesy bean hash, 103

chorizo and cannellini bean soup, 87

crusty Tex-Mex roll, 175

stir-fried steak chilli, 82

beef: boiled beef and carrots with herb dumplings, 247

dill pickle cheese burgers, 81

stir-fried steak chilli, 82

Thai beef salad, 209

thick-crust beef and stout pie, 141

Vietnamese beef noodles, 78–9

Bellini jellies, 268–9

biscuits: gorgeous cranberry cookies, 181

black-eyed beans: Boston baked pork and beans, 211

blueberry pancakes, 276

Boston baked pork and beans, 211

bread: butternut chowder with cheese toasties, 88

crusty Tex-Mex roll, 175

English breakfast salad, 33

hot lamb baguette with mint and lime, 203

Italian fried eggs, 23

Parma ham and mozzarella focaccia, 162–3

sausage, onion and mustard soda farls, 36

skewered lamb and aubergine pittas, 168

spicy omelette chapatti, 172

vanilla eggy bread, 34

broad beans: aubergine, feta and broad bean salad, 148

broccoli: long stem broccoli with chilli and lemon, 256

brownies, caramel ripple, 182

bruschetta, panettone, 275

burgers: butter bean and mozzarella burgers, 217

dill pickle cheese burgers, 81

butter bean and mozzarella burgers, 217

butter-roasted cod with spring onion mash, 58–9

butternut squash: butternut chowder with cheese toasties, 88

butternut squash and Parmesan muffins, 179

C

cabbage: crusty-topped shepherd's pie, 244

fusilli with cabbage and crispy bacon, 85

cakes: moist mango and maple cake, 189

rough raspberry and almond slice, 188

soggy belly chocolate fudge cake, 284–5

cannellini beans: chorizo and cannellini bean soup, 87

stir-fried steak chilli, 82

caramel ripple brownies, 182

caramelised pepper spaghetti, 97

carrots: boiled beef and carrots, 247

roasted carrots with garlic and parsley, 253

casseroles: boiled beef and carrots, 247

Boston baked pork and beans, 211

sausage and lentil casserole, 214

chapattis: meatball curry with, 139

spicy omelette chapatti, 172

cheese: aubergine, feta and broad bean salad, 148

butter bean and mozzarella burgers, 217

butternut chowder with cheese toasties, 88

butternut squash and Parmesan muffins, 179

cheese and onion baked potatoes, 153

cheese and tomato macaroni, 94–5

cheesy bean hash, 103

crusty-topped shepherd's pie, 244

dill pickle cheese burgers, 81

ham and cheese puffs, 171

mozzarella and tomato bagel melt, 32

pan-fried haloumi with fennel salad, 112

Parma ham and mozzarella focaccia, 162–3

Parmesan baked eggs and mushrooms, 25

potato pasties, 176

quattro stagioni baking tray tart, 230

red pepper and fontina cous cous, 152

roast salmon and goat's cheese salad, 222

smoked haddock and prawn pie, 122